Freezing

Pamela Dotter

Macdonald Guidelines

First published 1978
Macdonald Educational Ltd,
Holywell House, Worship Street,
London EC2A 2EN

ISBN 0 356 06026 8

Made and printed by
Waterlow (Dunstable) Limited

Contents

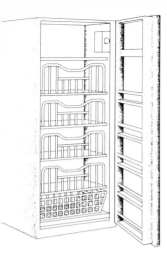

Preservation by freezing

The purpose of preserving food is to protect it from the causes of decay, thereby preventing it from developing unpleasant flavours, texture and appearance, during both preservation process and storage.

The causes of food decay

All food contains micro-organisms that continually alter it during its growth period. Micro-organisms are responsible for the changes that occur during maturing or ripening and eventually for the breakdown of the food. They cause loss of nutritive value and can sometimes also cause food spoilage and even poisoning. Micro-organisms and enzymes—protein substances that cause changes in the flavour and sometimes the colour of food—multiply quickly in warm, moist conditions.

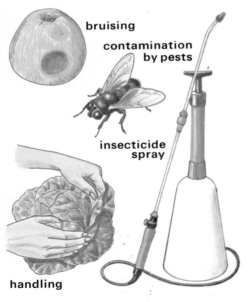

bruising

contamination by pests

insecticide spray

handling

Sugar, salt, vinegar, alcohol and sulphur dioxide are among the substances that inhibit the growth of micro-organisms and enzymes. All of them are used to preserve food, but they change the state of the food, as when fruit is preserved by being made into jam or chutney. Heat is used in conjunction with these substances, or on its own, to make possible a limited period of storage after cooking. In freezing, often both heat and cold are used: first heat, in the cooking of food or blanching of vegetables, then cold, in the freezing process.

Preservation by cold

The growth of micro-organisms is slowed down by cold. Storage time depends on the degree of cold. For example, a refrigerator running at about 4°C, 40°F will keep food for a few days. The same food stored in a home freezer running at —18°C, 0°F will keep for a few months. Freezing brings about some physical changes in food, which is why storage times vary. These changes are caused by enzymes.

Enzymes are still active at freezer storage temperature and must be destroyed by blanching before some foods are frozen.

The effect of freezing on food

Not all foods freeze successfully. The crystals formed in the food during freezing sometimes break down the structure of the

▶ How it all began: eskimos have always enjoyed the advantages of quick-frozen fish, though we may not envy them their means of retrieval!

4

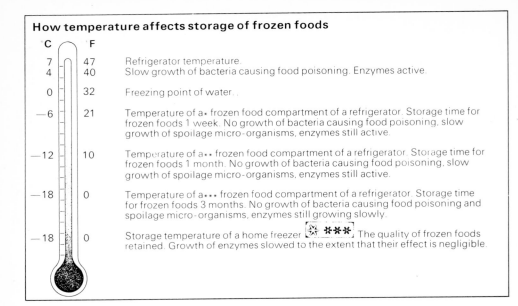

How temperature affects storage of frozen foods

°C	°F	
7	47	Refrigerator temperature.
4	40	Slow growth of bacteria causing food poisoning. Enzymes active.
0	32	Freezing point of water.
−6	21	Temperature of a∗ frozen food compartment of a refrigerator. Storage time for frozen foods 1 week. No growth of bacteria causing food poisoning, slow growth of spoilage micro-organisms, enzymes still active.
−12	10	Temperature of a∗∗ frozen food compartment of a refrigerator. Storage time for frozen foods 1 month. No growth of bacteria causing food poisoning, slow growth of spoilage micro-organisms, enzymes still active.
−18	0	Temperature of a∗∗∗ frozen food compartment of a refrigerator. Storage time for frozen foods 3 months. No growth of bacteria causing food poisoning and spoilage micro-organisms, enzymes still growing slowly.
−18	0	Storage temperature of a home freezer ❄ ∗∗∗. The quality of frozen foods retained. Growth of enzymes slowed to the extent that their effect is negligible.

food. Some foods, such as certain types of commercial yoghurt, and homogenized milk, are prepared in such a way that this effect is minimal. If in doubt about whether a prepared dish will freeze, freeze a small portion. The worst that can happen is that it will have an unpleasant texture; it will not cause food poisoning.

Foods that will not freeze

Salad vegetables The leaves go limp on thawing, and can therefore only be used in a cooked form, such as soup. Celery and tomatoes can be used cooked.
Bananas These go black unless mashed with lemon juice and frozen as a puree.
Single and soured creams These separate on thawing. The addition of sugar to made-up dishes containing cream helps them freeze better.
Milk The ice crystals that form on freezing upset the emulsion of the fats in the milk, unless it is homogenized.
Mayonnaise The emulsion is broken by

freezing and the oil separates.
Gelatine The structure of a jelly is broken by freezing and the jelly will 'weep'. Whisking and adding sugar helps gelatine desserts to freeze well.
Plain yoghurt This breaks down on freezing.
Fruit-flavoured yoghurts These freeze slightly better because sugar has been added. Yoghurts sold already frozen have been specially prepared.
Avocados These turn black when frozen whole but will freeze as a purée.

The effect of freezer storage on food

Food continues to develop during storage because enzymes are still present. This works to the advantage of some foods which actually have a better flavour after storage, noticeably strongly flavoured foods like game and curries which mellow, just as a fruit cake does in a tin. Other foods, such as fats, change for the worse owing to oxidation; these go rancid, which is the reason why fatty meats store for less time than lean meats.

Cauliflowers and peaches go brown after long storage; the pectin content of fresh fruits is reduced and more fruit is required when making jam. Spices and seasonings change in flavour after storage of three months. Garlic becomes unpleasant and is best added after freezing, if possible. To prevent these changes occurring, oxygen must be excluded from the food as thoroughly as possible by covering it with syrup or gravy, coating with glaze and removing air from the package. Vegetables should be blanched, excess fat removed from meat and over-long storage of food avoided.

The nutritive value of frozen foods

Frozen foods can hold their own when compared with fresh market produce. The freezing process does not destroy any nutrients in food, though soluble vitamins and mineral salts may be lost by blanching and in the drip that occurs after thawing.

Vitamin C, the nutrient found in most fresh fruits and vegetables, is very unstable; destruction is started by enzymes the moment the food is harvested. Blanching kills the enzymes; therefore, if vegetables are blanched and frozen within hours of picking, as commercially frozen vegetables are, the Vitamin C content could be higher than that in 'fresh' vegetables bought from the greengrocer. Speed is essential if food is to be frozen successfully.

The development of freezing

The advantage of keeping food in cool caves was discovered in very early times, long before it was realized that warmth and moisture were the causes of putrefaction. The use of ice was first recorded in China,

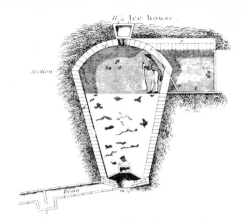

▲ Ice houses were built underground to provide insulation for the stored ice blocks.

but only for cooling drinks. At the beginning of the Christian era, Nero is said to have commanded his slaves to carry blocks of ice, to be used for cooling wine and food, down from the Alps. The use of ice as a preservative was then unknown because there was no means of keeping it.

The next development was the ice house. Excavations on the site of a first-century house in Austria have revealed an underground chamber fitted with racks for food and spaces for blocks of ice, with straw for insulation. In England, wealthy Elizabethans had underground igloo-shaped ice houses, situated near lakes so that use could be made of the frozen water during winter.

Next, scientists began to seek some mechanical means of producing and preserving a cold atmosphere. Many patents were taken out in the nineteenth century for the first developments in refrigeration. Meat-packaging plants were the first places to benefit from it.

In 1880 meat was transported from Australia to the UK in refrigerated holds. The storage life of food was longer, but still limited. Arctic temperatures were found to

keep food for longer than the new mechanical refrigeration producing temperatures of about 0°C, 32°F.

In the 1890s, the USA was leading the world in the development of refrigeration. The high summer temperatures and the country's growing population made refrigeration a high priority. In the early 1900s, an American explorer named Clarence Birdseye noticed that fish he caught in the Arctic froze solid and became coated in ice. The fish also tasted fresh even after it had been lying around on the ice for a few months. This told him, firstly, that the lower the temperature, the longer food would keep, and secondly, that food must be protected from the air to prevent it from drying: the coating of ice on the fish did this very efficiently.

Commercial freezing

The big breakthrough came in about 1930 when Clarence Birdseye came to the conclusion that the quality of the frozen food was vastly improved if it had been frozen quickly. Food is mostly water, and if it is frozen slowly large ice crystals form which break down the cell walls. When the food is thawed the moisture runs out together with some of the nutrients and

▲ Modern fishing trawlers have facilities for processing and freezing fish at sea.
◀ Clarence Birdseye.

flavour, making the food dry, tough and tasteless.

Quick freezing produces small ice crystals that do not distort the cells. In conjunction with General Foods of America, Clarence Birdseye patented a process to lower food in temperature from −1°C (30°F) to −5°C (23°F) in a matter of minutes, rather than the hours taken by the older methods of freezing.

The same principle of quick freezing is used today. With the development of refrigerated shelves for quick freezing of packs, blast freezing—blowing cold air through a tunnel—and freezing with liquid nitrogen came the possiblity of producing frozen foods commercially.

As the frozen food industry developed, advances were made in both freezing processes and storage. The advantages of freezing were illustrated by one of the most perishable foods—fish. Frozen fish, when first put on the market, was a new taste for most people. Its fresh taste was quite different from that of the strong flavour of the staler fish to which they were accustomed.

Frozen food processing plants were first built round the fishing ports, where they still thrive today alongside facilities for freezing other foods.

Home freezing

A freezer is simply an insulated box with refrigerant coils around the sides or built into the shelves. The coils are powered by an electric motor with a thermostat to maintain a constant low temperature. The first home 'freezers' were conservators from the ice cream industry.

They lacked the storage capacity of modern freezers and their design was not ideal for home freezing. The first real freezer was a chest design. Like today's freezers, it could fast-freeze food and store it at the low temperature required. Home freezers provide a fast-freezing process which freezes thin packs of food in about one hour; commercial appliances, which freeze within minutes, are still much faster.

The advantages of owning a freezer

Every family has different needs, but there are few who cannot benefit from the economies in time, money and effort that owning a freezer brings. With a freezer, waste can be eliminated: leftovers can be frozen, as can gluts of garden produce. Buying in quantity saves on shopping time, and bulk-buying usually means cheaper prices. Menus can be more varied as out-of-season foods will be available from the freezer. If a whole batch of single portions is frozen, catering for special diets or emergencies will be easier. Dishes cooked in double quantities will save time later.

Entertaining will be simplified, too, as food can be prepared in advance. Lastly, freezing is the simplest, safest and easiest method of food preservation.

▲ An insulated ice box, c. 1900.

▼ This 1914 refrigerator had three separate storage areas and an ice-making compartment, and was fan-cooled by the compressor motor on top of the cabinet.

Equipment for home freezing

The right choice of a freezer is important— and the bigger the better. Until a freezer has become a member of the family, it is difficult to imagine just how much it will be used. Remember that bulk packs are large and take up a lot of space. If you intend to buy meat, the best savings are in the large packs. Gardeners will need a large freezer to cope with gluts of produce. A large freezer is relatively cheaper to buy per litre than a small one.

Choosing a freezer

It is most important to make sure that the appliance carries the food freezing symbol:

This means that it is capable of freezing fresh food as well as storing frozen foods.

Appliances with only three stars, similar to the frozen food compartment of a refrigerator, will only store already frozen foods. These appliances, called conservators, are mostly used commercially for storing frozen foods and ice cream.

The manufacturer's instruction book and the rating plate on the appliance will indicate how much food can be frozen within 24 hours, without lowering the quality of the food already inside the freezer. The quantity is usually about one-tenth of the storage capacity.

Types of freezer Currently available are chest freezers with top-opening lids, upright freezers with one or two doors and a combination upright refrigerator/freezer with two separate compartments. The type chosen will depend on the space available, but if space is no problem, work out your requirements according to how you will use the freezer.

Choose a chest freezer for storing large packs of bought frozen food, for lower purchase price and lower running costs. Packing is more difficult, however, and small people find it impossible to reach to the bottom of a chest freezer.

Choose an upright freezer if you are not very tall, if you would find it easier to pack, or if you intend to freeze quantities of home produce (making sure your freezer has evaporator tubes in the shelves). Some upright freezers have an automatic defrosting mechanism with a fan to circulate the cold air.

Size A rough guide is to allow 120 litres (4 cu ft) freezer capacity for each member of the family. If you wish to store large quantities of home-grown produce you will need more.

How much does a freezer cost to run?

One unit of electricity is required for each 15 litres ($1\frac{1}{2}$–2 cu ft) of freezer space per week. It will cost slightly more if the fast-freeze switch is operated. Every time you open the door and let warm air in, you incur more electricity costs. Upright freezers lose the most cold air when they are opened, but as food is easier to find in these than it is in a chest freezer, this makes the running cost about equal. It is best to store food in plastic carrier bags in a chest freezer so that the bag can be removed quickly, the lid closed, the food found and the carrier replaced.

CHEST FREEZER

UPRIGHT FREEZER

Siting the freezer

Choose a cool, dry, well-ventilated place. The kitchen is not always ideal, as it could often be too warm. Moreover, freezers must be kept well away from cookers and boilers. Any well-ventilated corridor, cupboard or even a garage will do. Protect the freezer from condensation from a concrete floor by standing it on wooden blocks. There must be room for air to circulate round the freezer so that it works correctly. Check that the floor can take the weight; a fully-loaded large freezer is extremely heavy. An electric socket with a 3-pin 13- or 15-amp plug is necessary. Battery-operated warning lights or bells situated in the kitchen are useful if the freezer is in the garage (remember to change the batteries regularly).

Defrosting the freezer

Freezers need defrosting whenever there is a build-up of ice. This occurs about once a year with a chest freezer and twice a year with an upright.

It is best to defrost when food stocks are at their lowest, following this routine.

1. Chill blankets and newspapers, assemble insulated boxes (as used for camping) if you have any and clear the frozen food compartment of the refrigerator.
2. Disconnect the electricity supply and empty the freezer completely; place ice cream in the frozen food compartment of the refrigerator and wrap the rest together tightly in the newspaper and blankets or stack in the insulated boxes. For speed, wrap the baskets from a chest freezer without unpacking.
3. If the freezer does not have a drainage hole, place towels on the base to mop up the water. Place metal bowls of hot water in the freezer to melt the ice. Never use a hair dryer—this could cause electric shock. Loosen the ice with a plastic scraper. Collect the ice in a dustpan.
4. Wash the freezer in warm water to which a little bicarbonate of soda has been added. Dry thoroughly.
5. Switch on the electricity and return the food to the freezer. Make out a new inventory list of the contents and place the oldest packs in the most accessible place.

11

Servicing and insurance

Keep the service agent's number adjacent or attached to the freezer in case of emergencies. If there is a breakdown and the food (especially ice cream) is softening, keep the freezer closed and do not open it until the fault is repaired. Food will keep in a fully loaded freezer for four to five days. Re-freeze if the packets are still icy but remember to use them soon. If the food is fully thawed but still chilled, cook it and re-freeze. Many insurance companies will insure against breakdown.

Packaging

All foods in the freezer need packing to protect them from the drying atmosphere, to stop oxidation and the carry-over of flavours from other foods. Fragile foods need packing in rigid containers to prevent damage. Packing materials must be strong to be able to withstand the very cold temperatures. They must be vapour- and moisture-proof. There are many specialist firms offering a comprehensive range of freezer packaging.

Polythene bags These are cheap and re-usable if not pierced. Heavy-gauge bags of 150 to 250 thickness are recommended for long storage. Bags with coloured stripes are available for colour-coding frozen food. Air can easily be removed from these bags by using a straw, tube or vacuum pump. The bags are sealed with plastic or paper-coated wire ties, sometimes incorporating a label.

Cling wrap or freezer film This is one of the most useful plastics for wrapping. It successfully excludes air from awkwardly-shaped packages such as those containing

▼ A range of freezer packaging, including cling wrap, foil, plastic bags and wire ties, labels, freezer bags and plastic containers.

meat and poultry and is useful for over-wrapping pre-formed blocks and individual items. The thicker grade of cling wrap is adequate on its own; the thinner grade needs further wrapping but is useful to separate individual items in a polythene bag.

'Boil-in' bags These bags, made of a plastic that withstands both boiling water and freezer temperatures, are used for packing and heating food and are especially useful for stews and sauces. Single portions of a whole meal can be heated together in a saucepan – ideal for people living alone.

Plastic tissue This very fine plastic sheet is useful for separating pieces of food or protecting fragile food.

Aluminium foil This is useful for wrapping awkwardly-shaped items. Food wrapped this way can be steamed or baked straight from the freezer.

Aluminium foil containers There are numerous shapes and sizes, including pie dishes, pudding basins, cake 'tins', plates and large party-size containers, some with fitted lids. The food can be cooked, frozen, re-heated and served in these containers. They can be re-used if washed carefully. Acid foods should not be stored in aluminium or pitting will occur: use instead a plastic-coated type or line with plastic film.

Laminated bags Made from paper or foil with plastic linings, these are useful for liquids and purées.

Plastic containers These are the most expensive but also the most durable form of packaging. It is worth building up a stock of these. They have well-fitting lids, some with airtight seals. Seal the lids of any others with freezer tape. The containers can be written on with a waxy chinagraph pencil for quick labelling. They are the easiest packaging to use for fruits, vegetables, meat stews, sauces and purées. Square shapes are easier to pack than round ones. Large plastic containers are available in both squares and rounds for packing fragile cakes.

Free cartons Margarine, yoghurt and cream tubs and plastic bags and containers can be saved for packing food. Test them first in the freezer to make sure that they will withstand the low temperature. Containers from commercially frozen foods are good.

Seals and labels

Freezer tape This tape, able to withstand very low temperatures, is used to ensure that lids do not pop off containers in the freezer (this could happen if there is insufficient 'headspace' – see page 93).

Plastic-coated wire ties Rolls of this material are a cheap, effective and very convenient way of sealing polythene bags. Some incorporate labels.

Plastic ties These can be written on and used as labels. They are available in colours for colour-coding packs.

Stick-on labels These have a special adhesive that withstands low temperatures. Use a felt pen for writing on them.

Electric bag-sealer This is used for heat-sealing bags after pressing out the air.

▼ The plastic bag is pressed between electrically heated bars which melt the plastic and seal the bag.

Using a home freezer

To the new owner, a freezer seems enormous, and the task of filling its gaping jaws thoroughly daunting. However, one visit to a freezer centre, a session picking soft fruit and a single glut of vegetables from the garden will half-fill it. Some basic foods and some pâtés, flans and gâteaux for the next time you entertain will do the rest.

Value for money

Remember that a freezer uses electricity all day and all night. To use it wisely, and recoup running costs, store only foods your family likes and aim for a quick turnover of food. Although vegetables will keep without deteriorating for a year, there is no need to keep them that long. Work out the costs involved in picking your own fruit and vegetables to freeze, including petrol costs, and the time needed to prepare the fresh produce and the cost of fuel for blanching. Compare this with the cost of the commercial bulk packs to see if it is worthwhile. It may be more economical to bulk-buy from your local greengrocer.

Bulk-buying

Your family's eating habits will change once you have a freezer. Most families admit to spending about the usual amount of money but eating better. It is a great temptation to buy bulk packs of luxury items from the supermarket or freezer centre, so work out a shopping list before you set out, and then stick to it. Most freezer centres publish lists of prices and there is usually a 'bargain of the month'. Check how long the different foods store (see page 85) so that you are not filling your

freezer with foods that all need using by the same date. At first, buy small packs and aim for variety so you can assess the quality before spending a large amount of money. Try to buy all bulk purchases ready frozen (especially if buying meat): the slow freezing of a home freezer does not retain the quality in the same way as a commercial blast freezer, which 'quick-freezes'. Go to a shop where you can buy the meat fresh – it is easier to assess the quality this way. The butcher will cut and pack the meat as you wish, then freeze it.

Bulk-buying meat This is where many families aim to make their greatest savings. It is essential to understand what you are buying in a half-pig, half-lamb or side-of-beef pack and to realize how much space it will take up in the freezer. A side of beef weighs just over 100 kg (220 lb). This will completely fill a 283-litre (10-cu-ft) freezer. The side of beef would probably be an economical buy if you were to share it with another family. However, it would not be economical if some of the cuts were disliked. It may be best to buy a pack containing only the cuts you normally use. The smaller packs contain:

Beef forequarter Weighs about 60-75 kg (120-150 lb): chuck or shoulder, middle rib or shoulder, forerib or standing rib, stewing steak, mince, brisket, fat and bones.
Beef hindquarter Weighs about 60-75 kg (120-150 lb): topside, sirloin, top rump, silverside, fillet steak, rump steak, thin flank, leg of beef (stewing), fat and bones.
Topbit and rump Weighs about 25-32 kg (50-60 lb): topside, top rump, silverside, rump steak, fillet steak, beef skirt, leg of beef, fat and bones.
Side of lamb Weighs about 7½-10 kg

BEEF FOREQUARTER

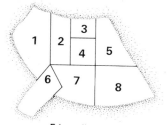

1 neck	**5** fore rib
2 steak meat	**6** shin
3 back rib	**7** brisket
4 top rib	**8** flank

BEEF HINDQUARTER

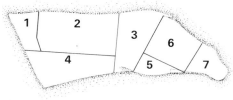

1 wing rib	**5** top rump
2 sirloin	**6** topside
3 rump	**7** leg
4 flank	

LAMB

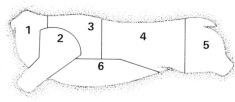

1 scrag	**4** loin
2 shoulder	**5** leg
3 best end	**6** breast

PORK

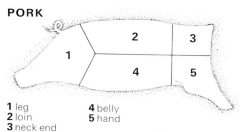

1 leg	**4** belly
2 loin	**5** hand
3 neck end	

(15-20 lb): one leg, one shoulder, one breast, stewing lamb, best-end-of-neck chops, chump and loin chops.

Side of pork Weighs about 22-30 kg (45-60 lb): two leg joints, sparerib joints, blade-bone joint, loin joint, hand and spring, streaky, trotters and half the head.

Remember that the price quoted per kilogram or pound is what a butcher calls 'dead weight'. By the time all the unusable parts are removed you will have lost between one-quarter and one-third, which is similar to the weight loss in fresh poultry.

Freezing home-prepared foods

Good-quality frozen food should be frozen as quickly as possible. (Freezing food in the frozen food compartment of a refrigerator is very slow, and spoils the texture and flavour of the food.)

Freezing food quickly It is important not to overload the freezer with unfrozen food or it will freeze slowly. The instruction book should indicate how much food can be frozen in any 24 hours.

The fast-freeze switch For the quickest freezing, operate the freezer's fast-freeze switch or turn the control to its coldest setting. Do this a few hours before the food is put in. This switch isolates the thermostat and gives continuous freezing power. It reduces the temperature from that required for storage to a lower temperature for freezing.

Freezing a full load will take from 18 to 24 hours and a half load from 10 to 12 hours. The fast-freeze switch can be switched off after 20 to 24 hours or 10 to 12 hours respectively. For freezing smaller amounts, dense foods such as fish and meat will take about 2 hours per $\frac{1}{2}$ kg (1 lb); liquids, vegetables, fruit and bread will take 1 hour per $\frac{1}{2}$ kg (1 lb). For freezing 1 kg (2 lb) or less, it is not necessary to use the fast-freeze switch. Chill the food in the refrigerator before freezing, pack the food in small thin packs and exclude as much air as possible. If there is air (a bad conductor of cold and heat) in the pack, it will prevent the heat being removed from the food. Suck out the air from freezer bags with a straw, rubber tube or vacuum pump. Place

the packs in a single layer with each pack in contact with a freezing shelf or wall of the freezer. Freezing takes place quickest if

the package is in contact with metal, not with cold air. Avoid stacking packs on top of each other and keep them well away from any already frozen food or they will take the cold from the food and not from the freezer.

The temperature of chilled food at 4°C (40°F) is 22°C (71°F) warmer than that already in the freezer—as different as temperature as warm water and hot water.

Freezing food in a single layer on a metal tray for a free-flow pack speeds up the freezing time, but the food can become dry if it is left exposed to the air too long. Aim to freeze only one tray at a time and pack the food as soon as it is frozen, in under an hour.

Packing the freezer

It pays to pack methodically so that you know where to find the food you need: the longer the door or lid is open, the more

Pack the freezer methodically so that you know where to find what you need.

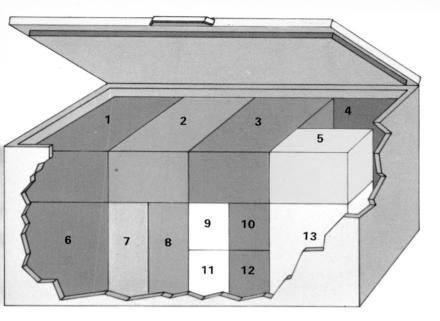

PACKING A CHEST FREEZER

1 Prepared meat dishes
2 Fruit salad, fruit in containers, desserts
3 Bread, baked foods, basic foods
4 Space for freezing own dishes
5 Ice cream
6 Joints and cuts of beef, pork, bacon; half a lamb
7 Fish
8 Fruit and vegetables in bags and large containers
9 Stock, juice, milk, dairy products
10 Leftovers
11 Cakes in boxes
12 Pastry
13 Compressor

PACKING AN UPRIGHT FREEZER

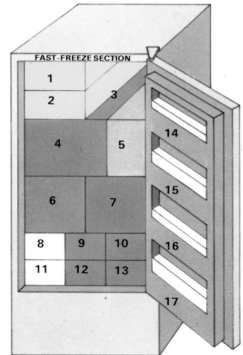

FAST-FREEZE SECTION

1 Desserts
2 Ice cream
3 Space for freezing own dishes
4 Prepared meat dishes
5 Fish
6 Joints and cuts of beef, pork, bacon, offal
7 Half a lamb
8 Small cakes, undecorated cakes
9 Pies, vol-au-vents
10 Bread rolls
11 Iced cakes in boxes
12 Pancakes, pastry
13 Bread loaves
14 Leftovers
15 Stock
16 Herbs, cubes
17 Fruit purée

Label each package clearly, or you may find yourself serving a fruit pie with vegetables and gravy!

cold air will be lost from inside the freezer.
Upright freezer This is the easiest to pack because it is just like a cupboard. Even so, small packets can become wedged and inaccessible. They are best collected together in large packs. Old nylons make useful containers for tiny packs of herbs and eggs. Allocate separate shelves for the various types of food (see page 17). It helps to colour-code the packs as shown.

Avoid keeping large boxes half-full of food; transfer the food to a smaller box.
Chest freezer Allocate space as above for different types of food. Colour-coding is even more helpful with chest freezers than with upright freezers. Use the baskets at the top for food to be used first. Keep food separate in the bottom by storing small packages in colour-coded plastic carrier bags or boxes that can easily be removed. Plastic ice-cream containers are useful for packing home-grown free-flow vegetables and fruit. They stack well and the food can be transferred to smaller containers as they become empty.

Labelling and recording

Label everything in the freezer, ensuring that the labels are firmly attached to the food packages. The label should state the kind of food, whether cooked or uncooked, the quantity or number of servings and the date of freezing. It is helpful to put cooking or re-heating directions on single portions of complete-meal dishes. Write clearly and boldly. Coloured paper labels can be packed into freezer bags and plastic containers written on with a waxy chinagraph pencil. Always label before chilling: labels will not stick to damp surfaces.
Record book Keeping a record of the contents of your freezer is invaluable. You can either make one from a card index system or ring file or buy one from a stationer's. Keep a page or card for each type of food and record everything you put in and take out.

Storage times

Given care in preparation, high standards of hygiene, good packaging and high-quality food, food should emerge from the freezer, even after a whole year, exactly as it was put into it. However, the enzymes which cause flavour deterioration and oxidation (it is impossible to exclude all the air from food packs) *will* very slowly destroy the flavour of the food and cause rancidity. Enzymes will never cause food poisoning, so the food will be edible even after two years' storage – but the flavour will have suffered.

In this book, the recommended storage times on page 85 and in the recipes guard against flavour deterioration. Fatty foods and fish are the most perishable, but as foods change in flavour during storage, it is best to rotate your food stock and use made-up-dishes within three months. Stack the new packets at the bottom of the freezer.

Thawing

Meat and poultry Joints and poultry must be thawed before cooking to retain their quality and to make sure that any harmful micro-organisms are destroyed. When thawed slowly, the meat is given the chance to re-absorb any liquid lost. Cook it as soon as it is thawed. Thin cuts such as steak or chops are best cooked from frozen. In an emergency, thaw the joint, still in its wrapper, in a bowl of cold water. It *can* be cooked while frozen but must be protected by a roaster bag, and a meat thermometer used to check when it is cooked. There will be a lot of 'drip' and consequently the meat will lose flavour and texture.

Vegetables and fruit These are best cooked from frozen and not left to thaw. Fruit often discolours on thawing. Soft fruit for serving raw is best thawed very slowly in the refrigerator. Pack so that it is easy to remove the right amount when you need it.

Baked foods It is usually best to thaw these, especially iced cakes and gâteaux, slowly in the refrigerator and cut while still firm. Bread stales quickly if thawed in the refrigerator or in the oven. It is best left at room temperature.

Prepared dishes These are best left to thaw in the refrigerator to save fuel in re-heating. A solid block of stew takes a long time to thaw and heat in the oven. The sauce may need beating well to return it to its original texture. Pies are best cooked from frozen for a good crisp crust. When thawing and baking at the same time, the food may be put into a cold oven and it will begin to thaw as the oven heats. Add 10 minutes on to the cooking time given for cooking in a pre-heated oven.

Thawing and re-freezing

If there has been a power cut, or if you have taken out food that is not required after all, it may be necessary to re-freeze the food. The action required depends on the state of the food.

Partially thawed food Dry the pack and quickly re-freeze.

Chilled pack, fully thawed Re-freeze bread, pastry, fruit. Cook meat, poultry and pies and re-freeze. Cook vegetables and, if they cannot all be used, make into purée or soup and re-freeze.

Warm packs, fully thawed Throw away all meat, poultry and vegetables. Throw away fruit if it smells 'off' or is fermenting. Cook and re-freeze if it appears wholesome, or use for jam or wine. Re-freeze bread and cakes if they smell fresh.

Label all the packs with the action taken and use as soon as possible. The flavour and texture will possibly have deteriorated, but the food will not cause food poisoning.

Freezing fruit

Best results are obtained when fruits are ripe but not mushy; make ripe fruits into a purée. It is not worth freezing damaged fruits. Fruit will keep for one year. All fruits, with the exception of bananas, will freeze successfully.

EQUIPMENT

Knives Avoid discoloration by using stainless steel knives for preparing fruit. Sharp or serrated knives and a potato peeler are also useful.

Sieve A nylon or stainless steel sieve is best for making purées. If you grow apple trees and expect windfall apples every year, an electric mixer with a sieve attachment could prove an investment.

Tray (for open freezing) Use metal trays that fit into the coldest part of the freezer and refrigerator for chilling before freezing. Baking sheets or Swiss roll tins are convenient, but must not be greasy. Plastic trays that stack are available for freezing but are not as efficient as metal: the freezing is slow and the fruit dries. For a small quantity of fruit, use an enamel plate or dish.

Ice-cube tray Use for freezing fruit purée and syrup.

PACKAGING

Freezer bags These are adequate for fruits with firm skins, such as plums and tomatoes. Use also to pack open-frozen fruit. Seal with plastic ties.

Cling wrap Use for whole, firm-skinned fruits such as citrus fruits. Pack in bags.

Containers Use plastic containers for freezing fruit in syrup and sugar. Large plastic containers (empty ice-cream tubs) are useful for storing fragile open-frozen fruit. Oblong or square containers are useful for pre-formed packs. Avoid using foil for very acid fruits as pitting will occur.

Waxed cartons or plastic beakers These are useful for fruit juices and syrups.

Ice-cube trays Use for fruit purées.

Chinagraph pencils Use for writing on plastic containers.

▼ Equipment for freezing fruit.

BASIC METHODS FOR FREEZING FRUIT

Open freezing

For free-flow packs, convenient for serving, open-freeze fruits that do not discolour and all soft fruits (except strawberries).

1. Operate the fast-freeze switch if freezing more than $\frac{1}{2}$ kg (1 lb) fruit.

2. Avoid washing fruit if possible; if necessary wash in iced water. Drain well and spread on kitchen paper.

3. Spread a single layer of fruit on a metal tray.

4. Chill in the refrigerator for $\frac{1}{2}$ hour.

▼ The three methods of freezing fruit: in syrup, layered with sugar, and open-frozen on a tray for packing in freezer bags. Blanch apple slices before open freezing.

5. Place in the coldest part of the freezer: in the freezing compartment of a chest freezer, or on the shelf on or near the freezing coil of an upright freezer. Leave for 1 hour.
6. Pack into plastic containers or freezer bags for storage.
7. Label and place in the freezer for storage.

In dry sugar
Use this method for juicy fruits that do not discolour, including raspberries, black-berries and loganberries.
   Use 200-300 g (8-12 oz) castor sugar to each 1 kg (2 lb) fruit.
1. Layer fruit and sugar in a large bowl. Turn gently to coat; pack into freezer bags or layer fruit and sugar in rigid containers. Leave 2 cm ($\frac{3}{4}$ in) headspace to allow for expansion on freezing.
2. Label, chill, then place in the coldest part of the freezer.

In syrup
Use for fruits that are not very juicy, such as apples, apricots, currants and peaches. This method is best for preventing discoloration, especially when acid is added to the syrup: use 30 ml (2 tablespoons) lemon juice, a 50-mg tablet ascorbic acid or 5 ml (1 level tea-spoon) citric acid to each $\frac{1}{2}$ litre (1 pint) water.
1. Make syrup using 250-500 g sugar to $\frac{1}{2}$ litre water ($\frac{1}{2}$-1 lb to 1 pint), adding acid if required; cool and chill.
2. Pack prepared fruit in containers.

▲ If the fruit floats, use some crumpled paper to hold it below the syrup.

3. Pour syrup over fruit to within 2 cm ($\frac{3}{4}$ in) of top to leave headspace.
4. If fruit floats, place a crumpled piece of grease-proof paper or plastic tissue on top to hold fruit under syrup.
5. Close container, label and chill.
6. Place in the coldest part of the freezer.

As a purée

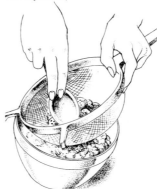

Use for strawberries, apples, berry fruits.
1. Cook fruit, if necessary. Press through a nylon sieve or liquidize, then strain out any fibrous material or pips.

Sweeten the purée to taste.
2. Pack as for syrup, leaving headspace. If containers are limited, remove from container then pack in cling wrap and a freezer bag.

Dry pack
Use for fruit with firm skins, e.g. currants (remove stalks after freezing), gooseberries (top and tail after freezing) and plums.
1. Wash fruit only if neces-sary; dry well.
2. Pack in freezer bags, label, chill and freeze.
To use Cook fruit from frozen.

Freezing fruit for jam and marmalade
Pack fruit for jam in weighed amounts but include an extra 50 g (2 oz) fruit for every 500 g (1 lb) packed to compensate for the slight loss of setting power of frozen fruit. Use a dry pack, as above, but if space is limited, cook the fruit, with-out sugar, and make into pre-formed packs (see pp. 36-37). Note the quantity, and the amount of sugar to be added, on the label.
   Wrap oranges for marma-lade in cling wrap, then pack in freezer bags. Label, chill and freeze.

Freezing fruit for wine
Some fruits for wine-making are improved by freezing because their texture is softened, making flavour-extraction easier. Pack apples, plums, elderberries, damsons, sloes, goose-berries and rose-hips in freezer bags.

Freezing vegetables and herbs

Only prime-quality young vegetables should be frozen. Mature ones can be used for soup packs or put in dry store. It is best to freeze vegetables as soon after picking as possible. If storing them for more than two weeks, they must be blanched, or scalded. Blanching destroys the enzymes that cause vegetables to discolour, and to lose their flavour and precious Vitamin C. To blanch vegetables, plunge them in boiling water for a few minutes, then cool quickly.

EQUIPMENT

Knives Avoid discoloration by using stainless steel knives for preparing vegetables.

Blanching basket Special wire baskets are available from suppliers of freezer equipment. If storage space is limited, buy one that collapses. A loose-mesh nylon shopping bag or wine-maker's straining bag can be used instead. Keep the basket or bag exclusively for blanching and wash well before and after use. The perforated separators from a pressure cooker can also be used.

Saucepan A large saucepan that will hold 3-4 litres (5-7 pints) of water with room to spare is necessary. A preserving pan or pressure cooker would be suitable.

Trays These are used for open freezing to make a free-flow pack. Use metal trays for the quickest freezing (make sure they also fit into the refrigerator for chilling).

Ice-cube tray Use for freezing chopped herbs.

Chinagraph pencil Use for writing on bags and containers.

PACKAGING

Freezer bags Adequate for most sturdy vegetables; large ones can be used for free-flow packs.

Containers Use these for fragile vegetables such as broccoli and asparagus. Large ice-cream containers are ideal for free-flow vegetables. Use oblong or square containers to make blocks of vegetable purée for soups.

▼ For blanching, use either a basket that collapses for storage, a nylon string bag, a wine-maker's straining bag or pressure cooker separator.

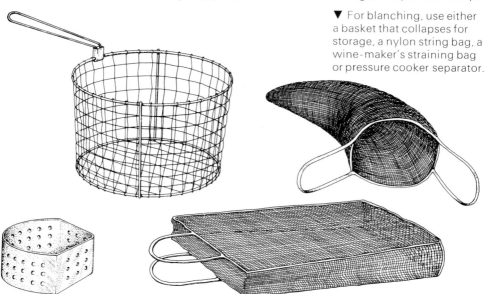

BASIC METHOD FOR FREEZING VEGETABLES

1. Operate the fast-freeze switch a few hours before needed. To avoid loss of flavour, cut runner beans into chunks.

2. Blanch $\frac{1}{2}$ kg (1 lb) vegetables in boiling water (for time, see chart on p. 89).

5. To open-freeze, spread in a single layer on a metal tray and place on freezer shelf.

6. Pack into plastic containers or freezer bags for storage.

3. Cool in iced water for a similar space of time.

4. Drain, turn on to a clean teatowel and pat dry.

7. If using freezer bags, pack usable amounts, remove the air with a straw, tube or vacuum pump, then close the bag and attach a label.

8. Place the packs in the coldest part of the freezer, isolated from any already frozen food until frozen.

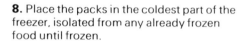

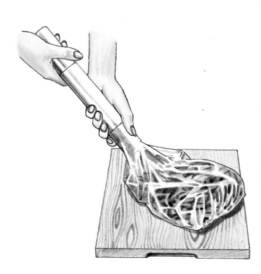

FREEZING HERBS

1. Pack sprigs of fresh herbs, without blanching, in freezer bags. To use, crumble the frozen leaves.

Add frozen to soups, stews and sauces; add vinegar to thawed mint cubes for mint sauce.

▼ Crumble the leaves of frozen fresh herbs on to cooked vegetables.

2. Fill ice-cube trays with chopped herbs, top up with water and freeze. For speed, chop herbs in a liquidizer with a little water. Store frozen cubes in freezer bags.

Problems affecting frozen vegetables and herbs

Ice in the pack	Caused by temperature fluctuation. Was the freezer bag punctured?
Shrunken vegetables	Air has entered the bag and caused dehydration.
Hay flavour	Vegetables were insufficiently blanched or have been stored too long.
Discoloured vegetables	Vegetables were blanched for too long or too short a time.
Soft vegetables	Vegetables have been over-blanched.
Musty herbs	Herbs have been stored too long.
Discoloured herbs	Herbs have been stored too long (blanch if long storage is anticipated).

Freezing dairy foods

Dairy foods are available throughout the year and can be stored for a reasonable time in the refrigerator. If space is short it is hardly worth freezing them, but an emergency stock is useful if you have the room, especially if the food is bought at a bargain price. Save waste by freezing leftover yolks or whites of egg, or pieces of cheese from a party cheese board.

PACKAGING

Use small plastic or waxed tubs, cling wrap or foil. Sterilized cream and yoghurt pots can be used, too.

METHODS OF FREEZING DAIRY FOODS

Eggs (whole) Eggs crack if frozen in their shells. Freeze as beaten egg in small containers in usable amounts: 45 ml (3 tablespoons) beaten egg equals one whole egg.

Egg whites Freeze up to four in plastic containers, or as single whites in sections of plastic egg boxes, or in tiny 50 g (2 oz) Tupperware containers. Remove and store in a freezer bag.

Egg yolks These must be mixed with salt or sugar. Add 2·5 ml ($\frac{1}{2}$ level teaspoon)

▼ Separate eggs and freeze yolks and whites separately.

salt or 5 ml (1 level teaspoon) sugar for each egg yolk and mix well. Pack as for whites.

Cream Freeze only pasteurized cream of 40 per cent butterfat content—that is, double cream or clotted cream. Whip double cream and sweeten for best results. Cream may be piped into rosettes on a foil-lined baking sheet, open-frozen, then packed into boxes. Place on desserts while still frozen.

Soured cream Do not freeze.

Butter Over-wrap butter with cling wrap or foil before freezing.

Cheese Soft cheeses such as Brie, Camembert and blue cheeses freeze well just over-wrapped with cling wrap or foil. Freezing retards the ripening, so make sure the cheese is fully ripe (it will ripen fast if placed in an

airing cupboard for a few days). Full-fat and medium-fat soft cheeses turn granular, but can still be used in cheesecakes. Hard cheese,

such as Cheddar, goes crumbly on storage. Freeze a bag of grated cheese for use in cooking. Use up thawed cheese quickly.

Ice cream Over-wrap bought ice-cream packets with cling wrap or foil. Pack homemade ice cream and sorbets in plastic boxes.

Yoghurt Homemade yoghurt does not freeze well. Some commercial yoghurts will freeze.

Milk It is not worth freezing milk, unless to avoid waste. Long-life packs are more convenient and save freezer space. Freeze only homogenized milk, packed in cartons; ordinary pasteurized milk separates on thawing.

Freezing meat, poultry and game

Meat stores well in a freezer. Make sure it has been well hung before freezing. For home freezing, choose only special cuts, specially prepared meat or real bargains of known quality. Buy the rest already frozen or any savings made will be cancelled out by the cost of the electricity required for freezing. Poultry freezes well and game improves in flavour when stored in a freezer, but freezing will not improve tough meat.

EQUIPMENT

Sharp knives are needed for boning and preparing meat. Ask the butcher to do the skilled part. A small saw is useful for trimming protruding bones such as the chine bone on lamb.

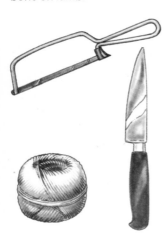

PACKAGING

Cling wrap Use for wrapping joints of meat and poultry.
Plastic tissue or grease-proof paper Use for interleaving slices of meat.
Foil Use for wrapping chops, steaks and chicken joints.
Plastic trays Use for stacking chops and chicken joints.

PREPARING MEAT FOR FREEZING

Freeze only 1 kg (2 lb) for each 30 litres (1 cu ft) of freezer space in any 24 hours. Cut off any surplus fat because it is the fat that turns rancid and reduces the storage time of meat. This is why lean meats such as topside of beef will keep longer than fatty ones such as belly of pork. Cut the meat into usable portions. If possible, remove the bones, which take up valuable space.

Boning

Meat with a high proportion of bone, such as neck of lamb, is best cooked first so that the bones are easier to remove. Use a small saw for trimming off protruding bones. Bone and roll or stuff joints of meat, especially best end and shoulder of lamb and shoulder of pork. Use delicately flavoured stuffings: herbs, spices and seasonings intensify in flavour during storage Roast, then boil or pressure-cook the bones to make stock (see p. 45).

Tie the meat with fine string, securing with a butcher's slip knot. Cut into joints of a usable size.

Preparing a best-end joint of lamb for the freezer

1. Bone the joint.

5. Make another knot and pull it tight.

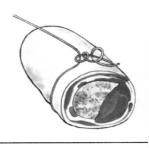

WRAPPING

Joints Cover protruding bones with a pad of foil, then wrap closely in foil, polythene sheeting or cling wrap to exclude as much air as possible. Fold over the two edges of the foil until they form a close seal. Turn in the sides, seal with freezer tape, label, chill and freeze.

Chops, escalopes, slices

Interleave with plastic tissue and wrap in foil. Pack in amounts suitable for a single family meal.

Wrap breaded escalopes separately in cling wrap. Press out the air before closing the package.

Mince Pack in freezer bags in usable amounts for the

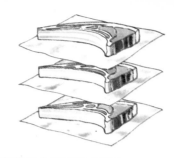

2. Place a roll of stuffing (see p. 51) along the joint.

3. Roll up the joint and tie with a butcher's knot (see step 4).

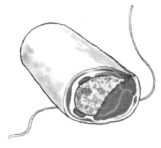

4. Wrap the string round the joint, loop one end round the other and secure with a knot.

6. Make a knot on the other side of the loop to secure.

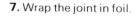

7. Wrap the joint in foil.

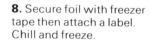

8. Secure foil with freezer tape then attach a label. Chill and freeze.

number of portions required. To save space, press into oblong containers to make 'bricks'. Remove and overwrap with cling wrap. Pack in freezer bags.

▼ A cling-wrapped mince 'brick' in a freezer bag.

Stewing steak Remove excess fat and gristle, cut into cubes. Pack in freezer bags in usable amounts for the number of portions required. Press into containers as for mince to make the meat easy to pack into the freezer. Make shallow packs for the quickest thawing. Thaw the meat before cooking. Freeze kidney separately.

FREEZING OFFAL
Freeze only when very fresh. Wash and dry well. Remove any pipes. Interleave slices of liver with plastic tissue. Pack in small amounts. Tripe should be dressed before freezing. Pack hearts separately in cling wrap. Add date of freezing to offal labels.

FREEZING POULTRY
Whole Prepare and draw, then wipe clean with kitchen paper. Truss with fine string (tie the legs together, then turn the wing tips underneath the bird, thread the string through the wing joints and tie securely).

Pad the leg bones with foil or greaseproof paper, then wrap in a freezer bag and exclude air. Pack the giblets separately in cling wrap and store at the side of the bird unless storing them for under 3 months. For longer storage, pack separately from the bird. Pack stuffing separately. For party dishes, bone, stuff and freeze whole chickens and turkeys, but store for only 1 month.

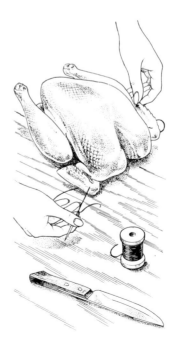

Joints Cover sharp bones, then wrap each joint in cling wrap and store in a freezer bag. Protect with a stockinette sleeve to prevent holes in the bag. If space is short, bone the joint.

FREEZING GAME
Game birds Hang game birds, (pheasant, partridge, grouse, woodcock, wild duck or wood pigeon) from the neck for at least four days before plucking, drawing and trussing. Leave longer if the weather is very cold and a strong flavour is preferred. Flavour will not develop after freezing. Pack as for poultry, but do not freeze the giblets. Cook mature game birds before freezing.
Rabbit Paunch and hang for one day. Joint, then wrap in cling wrap and pack in freezer bags.
Hare Paunch and hang for two days. Freeze as for rabbit. Freeze some of the blood in a plastic container for 'jugging' or making soup.
Venison Hang the carcass for five days. Wrap prime joints in cling wrap. Cook the other pieces.

Freezing fish and shellfish

Only really fresh fish should be frozen. It deteriorates very quickly. Ideally, you should find out when it was caught so that you can freeze it within twenty-four hours. Shop-bought fish is best frozen in fish pies. Shellfish deteriorates even more quickly and is only safe to freeze if it is known to have come from a reliable source.

PREPARATION OF FISH

To prevent deterioration, fish should be killed and gutted as soon as possible. On hot days it should be stored in an insulated bag.

Scale fish and remove fins, tail and head as for cooking the fish.

Fillets and steaks Make a salt solution by dissolving 30 ml (1 rounded tablespoon) salt in 1 litre (2 pints) chilled water. Dip in each piece, count twenty, then place on a rack to drain. This firms the flesh. Pack sufficient for one meal in each pack; separate each fillet or steak with plastic tissue, then pack in foil or a freezer bag. Remove as much air as possible, then chill, label and freeze.

Alternatively, dip in flour, egg and browned breadcrumbs as for cooking. Separate fillets with plastic tissue.

Whole fish A large whole salmon can form the centrepiece of a celebration meal. Whole codling or haddock can also make spectacular meals. Freshly caught trout can be frozen this way too. Scale and gut, but leave the head on the fish.

Glazing This simply means protecting the fish by covering it with a layer of ice. Do this for special fish. Chill the fish, then open-freeze as quickly as possible in the coldest part of the freezer. Have ready a bowl of iced water, sufficiently large to immerse the whole fish. Dip the fish: a layer of ice will form on the surface. Return to the freezer for 1 hour then repeat several times. Wrap in cling wrap or in a special salmon bag if storing for longer than two weeks.

OILY FISH

Oily fish include herrings, mackerel and trout.

Dip fillets and steaks in an ascorbic-acid (Vitamin C)

solution instead of salt solution before freezing. Use 20 ml (2 rounded teaspoons) ascorbic acid to each 1 litre (2 pints) water.

To freeze whole Prepare as for cooking, removing head, fins and backbone. Wrap tightly in cling wrap or foil. Cook foil-wrapped fish in its wrapping by baking or grilling.

SHELLFISH

Prepare and cook as for eating immediately.

Crab Pack white and dark meat separately, freeze the scrubbed shell for serving and some of the small legs for garnish; pack separately.

Lobster and crayfish Treat as crab.

Prawns and shrimps Cook and remove heads and shells. Pack a few unshelled separately for garnishing dishes.

Mussels Remove cooked mussels from shells; pack in plastic containers and cover with their own juice.

Freezing baked foods

Two cakes take almost the same time to make as one and baking two at once utilizes the oven heat very efficiently. It pays to get into the habit of batch baking. Bulk buying is also economical, especially if you can buy up a stock of baked food at the end of a day's trading. Nearly all baked foods freeze well; some even improve with freezing.

BREAD

Enjoy the luxury of always having fresh bread by storing it in the freezer. Thaw out each day's requirement, but be prepared for unexpected guests by keeping some sliced bread which thaws quickly or can be used frozen.

Bread from the baker Store a selection of loaves of bread, but include some sliced bread for immediate use. Separate the slices and toast or fry from frozen or leave to thaw for about 10 minutes.

Bread rolls Crisp rolls lose their top crust after freezing, but soft rolls freeze most successfully. Pack in freezer bags as closely as possible. A vacuum pump is particularly useful for soft bread rolls as it draws out some air from the rolls as well as from around them so that they take up less freezer space. They recover their

shape when removed from the bag. Over-wrap bread with cling wrap or place in a freezer bag. Waxed paper is adequate protection for storage up to two weeks; place in a freezer bag for longer storage. Part-baked rolls and bread freeze well.

Home-baked bread Making your own bread helps your freezer to pay for itself. Bread rolls are particularly economical to make. Experiment with different types of bread, mixing white and wholemeal flours and adding eggs and milk for enriched, soft-textured breads. Shape bread rolls into fancy shapes for maximum effect. Make plaits, tiny cottage rolls, twists, clover leaves and knots, and try making freezer rolls from bread dough (see p. 79).

Pizzas Save some of the batch of dough to make pizzas (see p. 79), which freeze well wrapped individually.

Yeast dough The uncooked dough may be frozen straight after the first kneading. Place in an oiled freezer bag, allowing space for rising (the yeast continues to make the dough rise until it is frozen). Freezing kills some of the yeast cells so double the amount of yeast in the recipe

if you intend to freeze the dough. It is advisable to cook or part-cook instead of freezing the raw dough.

Breadcrumbs Use up stale bread by making breadcrumbs and storing in freezer bags. Breadcrumbs are useful to have in the freezer, especially as they can be used when frozen.

PASTRY

All types of pastry freeze well. Pack in thin sheets to assist thawing.

Shortcrust Freeze rubbed-in mixture in freezer bags. Use frozen when required. Made-up pastries such as sausage rolls, mince pies and eccles cakes are best frozen after shaping. Open-freeze on metal trays, then pack in boxes when frozen. Glaze and bake from frozen, allowing 10 minutes more cooking time than usual.

Rich sweet shortcrust, as used for mince pies or fruit flans, is best filled and cooked before freezing as it is too fragile to remove from tins when raw.

▶ Have the components of fruit pies ready in the freezer. Store rolled-out pastry between foil and pre-formed fruit-pie fillings in cling wrap.

Pie crusts Roll out pastry to fit pie dishes and stack between sheets of grease-proof paper or foil. The pastry thaws quickly. Pre-formed fillings can be frozen to fit pie dishes. Moist fillings need thickening; coat fruit in a mixture of cornflour and sugar before freezing.

Flan cases Open-freeze un-cooked, remove the flan ring then wrap in foil.

To cook, replace in the ring, fill, then cook from frozen. Flan cases can also be frozen filled, uncooked or cooked.

Pies Make plate pies on enamel or foil plates. Do not cut the top crust, or the filling will dry out. Glaze and cook from frozen. Bake at 10°C, 25°F (one gas mark) lower than usual, and allow extra time for cooking.

If the filling could dis-colour, as it might in apple or peach pies, blanch the fruit first.

Puff pastry Freeze home-made pastry raw or cooked. Bought pastry can be re-frozen if shaped and cooked. Vol-au-vents can be cooked, filled and frozen if there is space. Heat from frozen.

Choux pastry Cook and

fill eclairs and profiteroles before freezing. Use sweet-ened double cream. Eclairs can be iced, then open-frozen. Pack profiteroles in freezer bags with a bag of separately frozen chocolate sauce.

CAKES

All cakes freeze well, but it is not worth taking up freezer space with long-keeping types, such as rich fruit cakes.

Plain cakes Wrap in freezer bags.

Iced cakes Open-freeze before wrapping. Unwrap before thawing.

Sandwich cakes Separate with greaseproof paper, pack in freezer bags. Fill with jam after freezing. Butter-cream- or double-cream-filled cakes can be filled before freezing.

Swiss rolls Roll hot, un-filled, with the paper inside. Cool, remove paper, then fill with butter icing or cream

and freeze. For jam filling, freeze unfilled, thaw then fill.

Gâteaux Freeze filled but with top undecorated if a cream and fruit topping is used. Butter-iced cakes can

be open-frozen and decor-ated before packing in boxes. Freeze whirls of piped cream separately and pack with decoration. Place on the cake and thaw slowly.

Biscuits Freeze uncooked or cooked. Raw dough is best shaped into a roll, wrapped in cling wrap, then partially thawed and sliced before baking.

Meringues No need to freeze, as they store for up to four weeks in a tin. They can be frozen but need packing in a box as they are very fragile. However, it *is* worth freezing meringue layers filled with cream or butter icing.

BATTERS

Make pancakes and cool on a rack. Stack between layers of plastic tissue and wrap in foil. Remove as required.

Heat in a frying-pan or thaw and fill with sweet or savoury fillings, arrange in an ovenproof dish and heat through.

Yorkshire puddings These are best frozen uncooked in greased individual tins. Re-move from the tins, pack in a freezer bag and cook from frozen when required.

Freezing prepared foods

Those who work full-time usually prefer the food in their freezers to be as near its finished state as possible. If you have cooked in bulk, you can take a frozen prepared dish out of the freezer, put it in the oven, set the automatic switch and have a meal ready when you arrive home from work. Dishes that are to be frozen should be slightly under-cooked and only lightly flavoured and seasoned. Those that incorporate potato, rice or pasta are particularly useful for storing.

PACKAGING
Plastic freezer bags These are very cheap, but are not suitable for liquids unless supported in some way to make a neat package.
Rigid plastic containers These are expensive but very durable. If used to make pre-formed packs, only a few are required.
Foil dishes and plates Use these when the food needs cooking.
Boilable bags Made from special material to withstand heat; food is frozen in them, then heated from frozen in a saucepan of water when required.

SOUPS
Vegetable soups freeze well; cream soups are best thickened with cornflour. Whisk during heating to counteract the slight curdling that occurs. Pre-form packs for freezing.

MEAT DISHES
Shepherd's pie, lasagne and moussaka can be prepared up to the final baking stage. Foil containers are useful for storing meat dishes. Otherwise, ovenproof dishes can be lined with foil: after cooking and freezing, remove and over-wrap the meat with more foil. Label the foil beforehand (including the number of portions and re-heating instructions). To use, peel off the foil and replace in the dish. Place in a cold oven, set the oven to moderate and heat for about an hour. Alternatively, thaw and heat according to the recipe.
Casseroles Thaw and heat in a saucepan, or thaw and heat in the original dish. Casseroles may be reheated from frozen, but this takes a long time and is extravagant on fuel.
Cooked meat For serving hot, pack slices of roast meat in containers. Cover with gravy to prevent drying.
  For serving cold, inter-leave slices with plastic tissue and wrap closely in foil or cling wrap.
Meat loaves and pâtés These freeze well. Turn loaves out of their containers and wrap in foil. Freeze cooked pâté in its dish; glaze and garnish after thawing.

PUDDINGS AND DESSERTS
Steamed puddings Make these in foil basins, cook, cool, cover, label and freeze. Thaw or heat from frozen.

Baked puddings These can be made in foil containers or in lined ovenware then removed and over-wrapped for freezer storage.
Trifles Freeze in ovenproof glass dishes or line with foil an ovenproof dish of similar size and shape to your trifle bowl. Freeze, remove from the ovenproof dish and over-wrap with foil for storage. To use, remove the foil and leave to thaw in the trifle bowl.
Mousses Freeze in individual plastic containers or jelly moulds. To use, de-mould and leave to thaw slowly.
Jelly This is not suitable for freezing. It becomes cloudy and 'weeps' because the ice crystals break up the structure. It freezes successfully if whisked, as the air bubbles cushion the ice crystals.

BABY FOODS
Save time and money batch-cooking sieved or strained foods for baby. Take extra care with kitchen hygiene. Pack in good-quality small plastic containers with lids, clearly labelled. Take out a day's supply at a time, thaw in the refrigerator, then place the covered container in a saucepan of water to heat.

BASIC METHODS FOR PRE-FORMED PACKS

Method 1

1. Fit a freezer bag into a square or rectangular box—an empty sugar box is ideal.

2. Fill with liquid, allowing headspace.

Method 2

1. Rigid, straight-sided plastic containers are ideal for pre-formed packs. There is no need to line the containers. Fill, allowing space for expansion, cover and freeze.

2. Press out the block from the underside, using the thumbs.

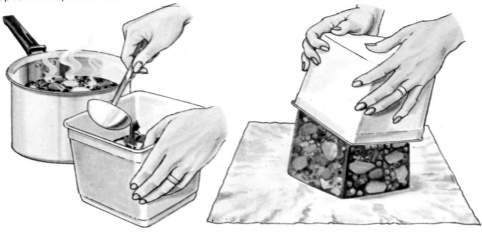

3. Close with a wire tie, chill, then freeze. Remove the frozen block from the box.

4. Label and store in the freezer.

3. Over-wrap the block in cling wrap, then pack in a freezer bag for storage.

4. If a special boilable bag has been used, place the bag in a saucepan of boiling water, then simmer until the food is thawed and heated.

Freezing leftovers

Freezing makes it possible to avoid waste entirely because all spare food can be frozen and utilized at a later date. Nearly all foods and made-up dishes will freeze. If you are unsure whether something will freeze, leave a small amount in the freezer until just frozen, then thaw it, keeping the remaining portions of food chilled meanwhile. Then taste your sample to decide whether it has frozen satisfactorily. It is unwise to re-freeze food which has already been frozen unless it has been cooked. Labelling each package and keeping a list of your stock is especially important. Unlabelled packages can cause great havoc! Keep small one-portion packages together in a freezer bag. They are useful for packed meals and snacks. Freeze as soon as possible. Cool hot dishes quickly and handle as little as possible.

MEAT DISHES

Sliced meat and poultry Even one slice of roast meat is worth saving; wrap it tightly in cling wrap and store in a freezer bag. If there is sufficient for one portion, make a tray meal.

Tray meals Use either a special foil tray with separate sections for meat, potato and a vegetable, or a large foil plate. Use cooked meat and cover with gravy to prevent drying; part-cook peas or beans, cool and place a knob of butter on top; or pack a frozen vegetable. Use well-flavoured mashed potato. Label a piece of foil, giving a description of the dish and heating instructions, and cover the dish. These tray meals are ideal to leave for the family to heat up when you are out.

Cooked meat pies and puddings These can be packed in small foil dishes or used for tray meals. Avoid open surfaces that would dry the meat.

Gravy This can be packed into small tubs or frozen in cubes.

Pâté Slice and separate with plastic tissue or grease-proof paper. Wrap in foil and press out the air.

▼ This meal in a special foil tray consists of sliced meat with gravy, sliced beans and mashed potato.

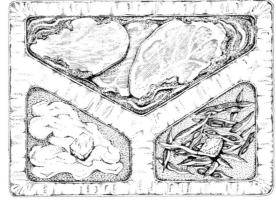

FISH
Make leftover white fish into individual fish pies or fish cakes—possibly with some leftover potato.

CHEESE
Leftover cheese from a party cheese board is best cut into portions that can be used up the day it is thawed. Pack in cling wrap and store in a freezer bag. Make sure the flavour of soft cheeses, such as Camembert and Brie, and blue cheeses has developed before the cheese is frozen.
Grated cheese Grate up ends of hard cheese and store in a freezer bag.

EGGS
Egg yolks Pack in small containers and mix in 2·5 ml ($\frac{1}{2}$ level teaspoon) salt or 5 ml (1 level teaspoon) sugar to each 2 egg yolks. Use savoury yolks for mayonnaise or rich sauces, sweet yolks for rich sweet pastry and custard. Label clearly.
Egg whites Pack in usable amounts in small containers. Egg whites can be whipped when thawed.

CREAM
Freeze as piped decorations (see p. 27) or make into ice cream.

VEGETABLES
Use green vegetables for tray meals or make into purée and freeze in cubes; add to casseroles, soups and sauces while frozen. Make into purée soups, possibly with leftover gravy. Mashed potatoes can be made into croquettes, or meat / fish

▼ Breadcrumbs can be made using either a cheese grater or a liquidizer.

cakes, used in soups or frozen as a pre-formed pack or in a boilable bag. Root vegetables, celery and onion can be packed as soup packs in freezer bags.

FRUIT
Use in pies or mousses. Grate orange and lemon rind and pack in small containers. Freeze juice in cubes. Freeze orange and lemon slices for drinks or garnish; separate slices with plastic tissue. Use frozen for drinks. Freeze single cherries in ice cubes.

RICE AND PASTA
Use up in cooked dishes or pack in usable amounts in freezer bags. To use, tip into boiling salted water, return to the boil, then drain.

BREAD AND CAKES
Make bread or cake crumbs and pack in freezer bags.

Pack buttered bread slices and slices of cake interleaved with plastic tissue. Wrap slices of French bread in foil. Place the frozen pack in a hot oven for about 15 minutes to thaw and refresh the bread. Wrap small cakes individually in cling wrap. Cut gâteaux into wedges, separate with plastic tissue or greaseproof paper.

STOCK AND GRAVY
Make bones into concentrated stock. Freeze stock and gravy in cubes or small containers.

DRINKS
Freeze leftover wine in cubes and use for cooking; add frozen to stock for casseroles or thaw and add to fruit cakes.

Basic foods to freeze

Victorian cooks owed much of their high repute to their kitchen maids, who did all the preliminary work of chopping, peeling, sauce- and stock-making, leaving the cook time to concentrate on finishing the dish. Stocking your freezer with prepared basic foods can give you a similar freedom.

CUBES
Small portions of liquid left-over foods or prepared foods that are required in small quantities (such as sauces) can be frozen in ice-cube trays, then packed in freezer bags.

Egg cubes Add a little water to beaten egg and store for when a small quantity is required for glazing pastry before baking.

Herb cubes Chop fresh herbs and half-fill cubes; top up with water to freeze. Alternatively, chop herbs in a liquidizer with water.

Sauce cubes Make mint sauce cubes as herb cubes. Mix a little sugar into the chopped mint and cover with boiling water; cool and chill before freezing. To use, add vinegar to thawing cube.

For white sauce, beat together equal weights of plain flour and butter or margarine and press into cubes. To use, place frozen cubes in hot milk and whisk until sauce thickens and boils.

Freeze apple sauce in cubes.

Fruit cubes Freeze un-sweetened sieved raspberry, strawberry, blackcurrant and tomato purées in cubes. Use for sauces or top up with fizzy lemonade for drinks. Mix grated orange and lemon rind with juice and freeze or just freeze the juice.

For party drinks, freeze cherries and pieces of can-ned fruit cocktail in cubes.

Stock cubes Make concen-trated stock (see p. 45) and freeze in cubes. Reduce the stock to concentrate the flavour either by boiling or by using a pressure cooker and only half the usual amount of water to cook the stock.

Wine cubes Freeze leftover wine (even the dregs, so long as they are not too muddy). Label clearly.

Baby-food cubes Small portions of purée are best frozen in cubes.

COOK-IN SAUCES
Basic sauces can be cooked in quantity and frozen in amounts of 250 ml ($\frac{1}{2}$ pint) in shallow blocks that will thaw quickly. When thawed, the sauce can be diluted and poured over raw meat, fish or poultry in a casserole for quick main-meal dishes. When the food is to be cooked in an automatic oven, the dish can be left in the oven to thaw for a few hours until the oven turns itself on. These sauces will store for up to three months.

Red wine cook-in sauce
Use with cubes of stewing lamb or beef, joints of chick-en, turkey or rabbit.
12 button onions or shallots
1 large onion
1 clove garlic
250 g ($\frac{1}{2}$ lb) carrots

FRUIT CUBES
blackcurrant purée

grated orange and juice

tomato purée

canned fruit cocktail

3 rashers unsmoked bacon
45 ml (3 tablespoons) oil
250 ml ($\frac{1}{2}$ pint) red wine
250 ml ($\frac{1}{2}$ pint) beef stock
30 ml (2 level tablespoons)
    tomato purée
10 ml (1 rounded teaspoon)
    mixed dried herbs
125 g (4 oz) button
    mushrooms
30 ml (2 level tablespoons)
    cornflour

Peel the button onions or shallots. Peel and finely chop the large onion. Peel and crush the garlic. Peel and slice the carrots. Chop the bacon, having removed rind and bone. Heat the oil in a saucepan and fry the button onions, chopped onions and bacon. Crush the garlic. Add the garlic and carrots to the pan. Cook for 5 minutes. Stir in the red wine and stock, bring to the boil and cook without a lid for 5 minutes. Add the tomato purée, herbs and washed mushrooms. Cover and simmer for 10 minutes. Blend the cornflour with a little water and stir into the sauce. Add salt and pepper to taste.

To use Dilute with half as much water. If necessary, thicken the sauce with extra cornflour just before serving. Garnish with green or black olives and serve with crisply fried triangles of bread.

To freeze As for white wine cook-in sauce.

White wine cook-in sauce

Use this sauce with fish, chicken, rabbit, veal, turkey or kidneys.
2 large onions
4 sticks celery

▼ Let frozen white wine cook-in sauce defrost over raw chicken in a casserole as it heats and cooks.

125 g (4 oz) gammon or
    bacon in a thick slice
50 g (2 oz) butter
1 lemon
250 ml ($\frac{1}{2}$ pint) sweet white
    wine or cider
250 ml ($\frac{1}{2}$ pint) chicken or
    ham stock
250 g (8 oz) button
    mushrooms
45 ml (3 level tablespoons)
    cornflour
salt and pepper

Peel and chop the onions, wash and slice the celery and slice the gammon or bacon. Cook in butter in a covered pan until the onion is soft but not browned. Stir in the lemon rind and juice, wine and stock. Bring to the boil, cover and simmer for 15 minutes. Stir in the mushrooms, return to the boil, then stir in the cornflour blended with a little water. Season to taste.

To use Dilute with half the quantity of milk and pour over the meat in a casserole. Stir in a little cream or top of the milk into sauce before serving. For a really rich sauce, beat an egg into 125 ml ($\frac{1}{4}$ pint) single cream and add before serving.

To freeze Pack the sauce into containers in 250-ml ($\frac{1}{2}$-pint) quantities, remove, wrap in cling wrap and store in a bag.

Tomato cook-in sauce

Use this sauce to serve with chops, chicken and burgers as well as to cook with them.
1 large onion
3 sticks celery (including
    leaves)
30 ml (2 tablespoons) oil
1 kg (2 lb) tomatoes or 2
    396-g (14-oz) cans
5 ml (1 level teaspoon)
    cinnamon
2·5 ml ($\frac{1}{2}$ level teaspoon)
    cayenne pepper
10 ml (1 rounded teaspoon)
    each of salt, sugar and
    mixed dried herbs
15 ml (1 tablespoon)
    Worcestershire sauce
1·70 g (2$\frac{1}{2}$-oz) can
    concentrated tomato
    purée

250 ml (½ pint) chicken stock
45 ml (3 level tablespoons) cornflour

Chop the onion, slice the celery, peel and halve the tomatoes. Cook the onion and celery in oil until the onion is golden brown. Stir in the cinnamon, cayenne pepper, salt, sugar, herbs and Worcestershire sauce, then the tomatoes and purée. Cook until reduced and pulpy. Press through a sieve, then add the stock blended with cornflour. Bring to the boil, stirring. Cover and cook for 5 minutes. Taste and adjust seasoning if necessary.

To use Dilute with half as much water. Add a blanched, sliced green pepper, if desired.

To freeze As for sweet and sour sauce.

Sweet and sour cook-in sauce

Pep up chops and chicken joints by cooking in this sauce, which can also be served with grilled meats. Serve with rice or noodles.

2 large onions
2 cloves garlic
45 ml (3 tablespoons) oil
1 small (170-g, 6-oz) can tomatoes
125 ml (¼ pint) malt vinegar
1 small (234-g, 8-oz) can pineapple slices
10 ml (1 rounded teaspoon) salt
pepper
45 ml (3 level tablespoons) sugar
10 ml (1 rounded teaspoon) made mustard
30 ml (2 tablespoons) soy or Worcestershire sauce

1 chicken extract cube
125 ml (¼ pint) boiling water
30 ml (2 level tablespoons) cornflour
1 green pepper

Chop the onions and garlic; fry in oil until golden brown. Add the tomatoes, vinegar, syrup from the can of pineapple, salt, a good shake of pepper, mustard, soy or Worcestershire sauce and an extract cube dissolved in water. Bring to the boil, cover and simmer for ½ hour. Blend the cornflour with a little water and stir in. Slice the pepper, having removed the core, and place in a saucepan. Cover with water,

bring to the boil, then drain, add the pepper to the sauce.

To use Dilute the sauce with half as much water, place in a casserole or saucepan with uncooked meat or poultry. Cook until tender.

To freeze Pack in containers, label, cool, chill then freeze. Remove block, wrap in cling wrap then place in bags to store (to make preformed packs, see pp. 36-7). Store for up to 3 months.

Curry cook-in sauce

This recipe makes a medium-hot aromatic sauce. To adjust the strength, vary the amount of ginger and black and cayenne pepper. If time is short, use 30 ml (2 level tablespoons) curry powder (double for hot curry) instead of mixing the various spices.

2 large onions
3 cloves garlic
30 ml (2 tablespoons) oil
5 ml (1 level teaspoon) each of ground cinnamon, turmeric and ginger
10 ml (2 level teaspoons) each of ground coriander and cumin
15 ml (1 level teaspoon) each of salt and sugar
2·5 ml (½ level teaspoon) ground black pepper
1·25 ml (¼ level teaspoon) cayenne pepper
3 large tomatoes
1 medium-sized cooking apple
1 chicken extract cube
75 g (3 oz) desiccated coconut
30 ml (2 level tablespoons) cornflour
135 ml (¼ pint) natural yoghurt

Peel and chop the onion and garlic. Place in a saucepan with the oil, spices, salt and sugar. Fry over a low heat, stirring occasionally, for 15 minutes. Skin and chop the tomatoes. Peel, core and chop the apple. Add to the pan and cook until pulpy. Dissolve the extract cube in 300 ml ($\frac{1}{2}$ pint) boiling water, add to the pan, cover and simmer for $\frac{1}{2}$ hour. Meanwhile, place the coconut in a bowl, add 300 ml ($\frac{1}{2}$ pint) water and leave for $\frac{1}{2}$ hour. Squeeze the coconut between the hands to extract the flavour, then strain. Add liquid to pan. Blend the cornflour with a little water and add to the pan. Bring to the boil, stirring. Cook for 5 minutes. Remove from the heat and add the yoghurt.

To use Dilute the sauce with half as much water, place in a casserole or saucepan with uncooked meat, poultry or fish, and cook until tender. Serve with cucumber, grated coconut, pineapple, chutney, bananas tossed in poppadums, lemon juice and yoghurt.

To freeze As for sweet and sour sauce.

Brown onion cook-in sauce

Cook mince, braising steak or liver and kidneys in this rich sauce.

4 large onions
2 sticks celery
60 ml (4 tablespoons) oil
10 ml (1 rounded teaspoon) sugar
45 ml (3 level tablespoons) plain flour

10 ml (1 rounded teaspoon) mixed dried herbs
30 ml (2 tablespoons) Worcestershire sauce
60 ml (4 tablespoons) sherry
2 strips orange rind
1 bay leaf
salt and pepper
$\frac{1}{2}$ litre (1 pint) beef stock

Peel and coarsely chop the onions. Wash and finely chop the celery. Cook slowly in the oil, with the sugar added, until golden brown; remove from the pan with a draining spoon; reserve. Stir the flour into the fat remaining in pan; add the herbs, Worcestershire sauce, sherry, finely chopped orange rind, bay leaf, 10 ml (1 rounded teaspoon) salt, some pepper and stock. Bring to the boil, stirring, cover and simmer for $\frac{1}{2}$ hour. Remove the bay leaf, replace the onion and celery and check the seasonings.

To use Dilute with half the quantity of water or stock.

To freeze As for sweet and sour sauce.

PANCAKES

Makes 16-20
200 g (8 oz) plain flour
2·5 ml ($\frac{1}{2}$ level teaspoon) salt

2 eggs
$\frac{1}{2}$ litre (1 pint) milk and water mixed
oil or lard

Place the flour and salt in a bowl, break the eggs into the centre and gradually mix in half the liquid. Beat until smooth, then add the remaining liquid. Or liquidize the eggs, salt, flour and liquid until smooth. Pour into a jug. Heat a little oil or lard to just grease a 15-20-cm (6-8-in) frying-pan. Pour in just enough batter to coat the bottom of the pan, swirl quickly then cook over a low heat until browned on the underside. Toss or turn with a palette knife and brown the other side. Cool on a wire rack. Use the remaining batter to make more pancakes.

To use Fill with various sweet and savoury fillings, such as thawed fruit purée cubes thickened with cornflour, or basic mince. Or reheat in the frying-pan with oil or a sauce.

To freeze Layer between greaseproof paper or plastic tissue and pack in foil. Label, chill and freeze. Remove as required, leave to thaw.

Soups

It is just as easy, and certainly much cheaper, to have a store of soups in the freezer instead of the cupboard. Vegetable soups are better frozen than canned because freezing retains the fresh flavours and textures. The basis of a good soup is tasty stock, which can be made from any surplus bones, poultry carcasses and vegetables. A pressure cooker makes this very easy. Use up all surplus vegetables in soups.

Pictured here are kidney soup with tiny choux buns, thick bacon and lentil soup, creamy onion soup garnished with crisp croûtons and minestrone.

TO FREEZE SOUPS

Slightly undercook and under-season. If cream is required, add it just before serving. Pack the soup in rigid plastic containers. If containers are limited, make pre-formed packs. Allow headspace. Label, chill and freeze for up to 3 months.

To thaw It is best to thaw soup at room temperature for several hours. Or heat slowly in a covered saucepan. Whisk thick soups lightly before serving.

SOUP RECIPES
Bone stock
meat, bacon, poultry bones or giblets, preferably roasted
1 large onion, roughly chopped
4 cloves
celery or celery leaves
root vegetables or washed peelings
fresh or dried herbs
12 peppercorns

Place all ingredients in a saucepan. Cover with water and bring to the boil. Skim, then cover and simmer for 2 hours. Strain, return to the pan, then boil rapidly to reduce by one-third. Alternatively, place in a pressure cooker, half-cover with water and cook at high (15-lb) pressure for 40 minutes; strain, cool quickly in iced water, chill, then skim.

To freeze Pour into ice-cube trays (see p. 40) or containers in usable amounts. Allow headspace. Remove blocks, cover with cling wrap, then pack in freezer bags. Store for up to 4 months.

To use Unwrap and thaw in a bowl in the refrigerator or heat slowly in a saucepan.

Creamy onion soup
Serves 8
1 kg (2 lb) onions
1 large potato
2 chicken stock cubes
75 g (3 oz) butter
75 g (3 oz) plain flour
$\frac{1}{2}$ litre (1 pint) milk

Peel and cut up the onions and potato. Place in a saucepan with $\frac{1}{2}$ litre (1 pint) water and stock cubes, bring to the boil, cover and simmer for 20 minutes. Pour into a liquidizer and blend until smooth. Mash butter and flour together on a plate, add to the goblet with some salt, pepper and celery salt. Return to the saucepan, add the milk and bring to the boil, stirring. Serve with crisply fried croûtons or onion rings. For a snack, serve with toasted cheese sandwiches.

Fresh tomato soup
Serves 10-12
2 large onions
4 sticks celery
100 g (4 oz) butter
100 g (4 oz) smoked streaky bacon
2 kg (4 lb) tomatoes
10 ml (1 rounded teaspoon) each of salt, sugar, mixed herbs and cinnamon
cornflour

Chop the onions and celery; cook in a covered pan with butter and chopped bacon for 10 minutes. Put the tomatoes in a bowl, pour boiling water over, count ten, then drain and remove

the skins. Cut the tomatoes into quarters then add to the pan with the salt, sugar, cinnamon and herbs. Cook without a lid until the tomatoes are thick and pulpy. Add an equal amount of stock or, if freezer space is short, cool without adding stock, pack into containers and freeze.

To use Thaw, add an equal amount of stock, bring to the boil and thicken with cornflour. Adjust the seasoning if necessary. Sieve or liquidize the soup.

Kidney soup
Serves 10-12
2 large onions
50 g (2 oz) lard
10 ml (1 rounded teaspoon) sugar
100 g (4 oz) fat bacon
250 g ($\frac{1}{2}$ lb) ox kidney
2·5 ml ($\frac{1}{2}$ level teaspoon) mixed dried herbs
1 small (70-g, 2$\frac{1}{2}$-oz) can tomato purée
2 litres (4 pints) beef stock
salt and pepper
red wine (optional)
50 g (2 oz) cornflour

Fry the sliced onions in lard with sugar and bacon until golden brown; remove from the pan. Remove core from kidney, cut into small pieces and fry in fat remaining in pan. Return the onions and bacon to the pan, add the herbs, tomato purée, stock and some salt and pepper. Bring to the boil, cover and simmer for $\frac{1}{2}$ hour. Liquidize until smooth in 2-3 batches. Blend the cornflour in the saucepan with a little water, add the soup, bring to the boil and cook for 2 minutes. Adjust seasonings if necessary.

To serve Add 15 ml (1 tablespoon) red wine for each portion, if desired.

To freeze Chill, make preformed packs, freeze and store for up to 2 months.

Bacon and lentil soup

Serves 10-12

1 smoked bacon knuckle
250 g (8 oz) red lentils
2 large onions
2 large carrots
2·5 ml ($\frac{1}{2}$ level teaspoon) mixed dried herbs
$\frac{1}{2}$ litre (1 pint) milk
45 ml (3 level tablespoons) cornflour
salt and pepper

Wash the knuckle and place in a pressure cooker with the lentils, peeled onions and carrots. Add 2 litres (4 pints) water, cover, bring to the boil, skim, then cook at high (15-lb) pressure for 25 minutes (or in a covered saucepan, with 3 litres water for 1$\frac{1}{2}$ hours). Remove the knuckle, peel off the skin and bone the meat. Replace the skin and bones in the pressure cooker or saucepan and cook at high (15-lb) pressure for 10 minutes or boil for $\frac{1}{2}$ hour. Cut up the meat. Discard the bones and skin, place the contents of the pan with the meat in a liquidizer and liquidize until smooth (or sieve the contents of the pan and add the meat minced).

To freeze As for kidney soup.

To use Thaw, then add herbs and milk blended with cornflour. Bring to the boil, stirring. Taste and season.

Minestrone soup

Serves 8

50 g (2 oz) haricot beans
2 onions
3 sticks celery
3 carrots
1 large potato
250 g (4 oz) streaky bacon
15 ml (1 tablespoon) oil
30 ml (1 rounded tablespoon) tomato purée
salt and pepper
2·5 ml ($\frac{1}{2}$ level teaspoon) mixed dried herbs
2 litres (4 pints) chicken stock
50 g (2 oz) shredded cabbage
50 g (2 oz) peas or green beans

Peel and chop the onions, wash and slice the celery, peel the carrots and potatoes and cut into small cubes. Soak the beans for several hours or pressure-cook for 10 minutes. Remove the rind and bone from the bacon, then slice. Fry the bacon in oil in a large saucepan, add the beans and vegetables and fry until the onion is lightly browned. Stir in the tomato purée, herbs seasonings and stock; cover and simmer for $\frac{1}{2}$ hour.

To use Add cabbage, peas or beans, cook for 10 min-

▼ How to dice carrots.

utes then thicken with cornflour blended with water. Serve with grated Parmesan cheese.

Note Add a crushed clove of garlic with the vegetables if serving straight away. Add garlic salt just before serving, if frozen.

Cream of cucumber soup

Serves 4-6

$\frac{1}{2}$ kg (1 lb) cucumber
2 shallots or 1 small onion
50 g (2 oz) butter
1 litre (2 pints) chicken stock
2 medium-sized potatoes
salt and pepper
125 ml ($\frac{1}{4}$ pint) thin cream or evaporated milk

Peel and chop the cucumber and shallots or onion. Melt the butter in a saucepan, add the vegetables, cover and cook over a low heat, shaking the pan occasionally, for 10 minutes. Add the stock, peeled and sliced potatoes, 5 ml (1 level teaspoon) salt and a shake of pepper. Cook until the vegetables are tender, then make a purée in a liquidizer or a sieve. Cool, chill and freeze.

To use To serve hot, bring to the boil, taste and add more seasonings, if necessary. Thicken with a little cornflour blended with milk, if desired. Stir in cream or evaporated milk, garnish with rings of fresh cucumber and serve immediately with croûtons.

To serve cold Whisk the soup when thawed. Whisk in cream (not evaporated milk). Adjust the seasoning and serve garnished with cucumber rings.

Snacks and starters

A selection of snacks and starters in the freezer is invaluable for casual meals. It is worth taking the time to pack the snacks individually so that it is no trouble to prepare a single portion. Entertaining will go more smoothly if you have the starter made in advance so that it only needs thawing out. Many of the dishes in this chapter are ideal for cold buffet meals and for packed meals.

VOL-AU-VENTS

Most freezer centres sell uncooked vol-au-vents, so it is hardly worth making your own, though a selection of frozen fillings in the freezer is useful.

Chicken and sweet corn filling

Fills 12 snack-size or 24 tiny cooked cases

1 (7-oz, 200-g) can sweet corn niblets
milk
1 chicken stock cube
25 g (1 oz) soft margarine
25 g (1 oz) plain flour
salt and pepper
250 g (8 oz) cooked chicken
125 g (4 oz) cooked ham

Drain the sweet corn into a measuring jug, and make up to 250 ml (½ pint) with milk. Bring to the boil and stir in the stock cube. Remove from heat. Blend the margarine and flour on a plate, add to the saucepan and whisk until smooth. Bring to the boil, stirring, cook for 2 minutes, then taste and add salt and pepper. Stir in the sweet corn, chopped chicken and diced ham.

To freeze Pack into tubs or containers or use to fill cooked pastry cases. Store for up to 2 months.

To thaw Leave at room temperature for 3 hours or overnight in the refrigerator. Beat briskly during heating.

Kidney and bacon filling

Fills 12 snack-size or 24 tiny cooked cases

100 g (4 oz) smoked streaky bacon
250 g (8 oz) kidney
1 small onion
250 ml (½ pint) beef stock
2·5 ml (½ level teaspoon) mixed herbs
25 g (1 oz) cornflour
30 ml (2 tablespoons) sherry
gravy browning
salt and pepper

Remove the rind and bone from the bacon; cut the bacon into small pieces. Remove the core from the kidney; cut the kidney into small pieces. Peel and chop the onion. Fry the bacon and onion in a saucepan until fat runs, add the kidney and cook, stirring, for 5 minutes. Add stock and herbs, bring to the boil, cover and simmer for ½ hour.

Blend the cornflour with the sherry, add to the pan and stir until thickened. Taste and add salt and pepper. Add some gravy browning. Pack, freeze and thaw as above.

Smoked haddock filling

Fills 12 snack-size or 24 tiny cooked cases

1 (227-g, 8-oz) pack boil-in-the-bag smoked haddock fillets
25 g (1 oz) long-grain rice
250 g (8 oz) cream or curd cheese
30 ml (2 tablespoons) lemon juice
45 ml (3 level tablespoons) mayonnaise
50 g (2 oz) gherkins or pickled cucumber

Cook the haddock as directed on the packet and drain into a saucepan. Place the fillets on a plate and remove the skin; flake with a fork. Add the rice to the fish stock with 4 tablespoons water. Cover and cook until the rice has absorbed the liquid and is tender (add more water, if necessary). Place the cheese in a basin, beat in the lemon juice, mayonnaise and chopped gherkins or cucumber. Mix in the rice and fish and add pepper to taste. Pack, freeze and thaw as above.

PATÉS AND TERRINES

Quick liver pâté

Serves 6

250 g ($\frac{1}{2}$ lb) fat unsmoked
  bacon
1 onion
250 g ($\frac{1}{2}$ lb) lamb's liver
25 g (1 oz) butter
15 ml (1 level tablespoon)
  plain flour
125 ml ($\frac{1}{4}$ pint) milk
5 ml (1 level teaspoon) salt
black pepper

Remove rind and bone from bacon, and cut the bacon into strips. Peel and slice the onion, slice the liver. Fry the bacon until fat runs then add the onion and cook until golden brown. Fry the liver until firm. Remove from the pan with a draining spoon and place in a liquidizer. Add the butter to the pan, then stir in flour, milk, salt and a generous amount of black pepper. Bring to the boil, stirring, then pour into a liquidizer. (If using a small liquidizer, make two batches with half of meat and half of sauce.) Liquidize until the mixture is smooth. Pour into a deep 1-litre (1$\frac{3}{4}$-pint) ovenproof dish. Place the dish in a tin containing 2·5 cm (1 in) of water and bake in a moderate oven (180°C, 350°F/Gas 4) for $\frac{1}{2}$ hour.

To serve Garnish with lemon and cucumber.

To freeze Turn out of dish, wrap in foil, label, chill and freeze. Store for 2 months.

To use Unwrap, replace in the dish and leave to thaw.

Country terrine

(see p. 76)
For a party, use one dish.
Serves 20

250 g ($\frac{1}{2}$ lb) lean pork or veal
$\frac{1}{2}$ kg (1 lb) minced belly pork
$\frac{1}{2}$ kg (1 lb) minced stewing
  beef
250 g ($\frac{1}{2}$ lb) minced bacon
250 g ($\frac{1}{2}$ lb) minced pig's
  liver
1 clove garlic, crushed
5 ml (1 level teaspoon)
  allspice
15 ml (1 tablespoon) lemon
  juice
45 ml (3 tablespoons)
  brandy or sherry
salt and pepper
3 bay leaves

Mix all the ingredients with 15 ml (1 level tablespoon) salt and six generous grinds of black pepper. Press into a 1$\frac{1}{2}$-litre (3-pint) deep round ovenproof dish and press the bay leaves over the surface. Cover lightly with foil or a lid and place in a roasting tin containing 2·5 cm (1 in) of water. Bake in a moderate oven (180°C, 350°F/Gas 4) for 1$\frac{1}{2}$ hours. Remove foil or lid and bay leaves and place a plate or cake tin base with a weight on top.

To serve Garnish with lemon slices, stuffed olives and bay leaves. Coat with aspic made by dissolving 5 ml (1 level teaspoon) gelatine in 125 ml ($\frac{1}{4}$ pint) beef stock.

To freeze Leave in the dish, if possible; cover with foil. Store for up to 2 months.

To thaw Leave in the refrigerator overnight or thaw for 6 hours.

Smoked mackerel pâté

This quickly-made pâté is ideal for entertaining. Use within six weeks.
Serves 12

3 slices bread from a large
  loaf
60 ml (4 tablespoons) milk
3 smoked mackerel
$\frac{1}{2}$ a lemon
100 g (4 oz) cream cheese
30 ml (2 tablespoons)
  mayonnaise
100 g (4 oz) butter, melted

After discarding the crusts, break up the bread and place it in a basin with the milk. Mash with a fork. Remove the skin and bone from the mackerel; flake the fish with a fork. Scrub the lemon, grate the rind finely and squeeze out the juice. Add the bread and mix well. Beat the cream cheese, mayonnaise and butter together. Beat into the bread mixture with the mackerel. Add salt and pepper to taste. Pack into individual pots or a soufflé dish, or mould in foil tartlet cases. Press out when frozen then pack in foil.

To serve Garnish with lemon and serve with hot toast and butter.

Salmon seafood pâté

(see p. 73)
This pâté can be made quickly and set in individual containers, in a soufflé dish or in a foil container.
First layer:

1 212-g (7$\frac{1}{2}$-oz) can pink
  salmon
15 ml (1 level
  tablespoon) tomato
  ketchup
15 ml (1 tablespoon)
  lemon juice
100 g (4 oz) full-fat soft
  cream cheese
2·5 ml ($\frac{1}{2}$ level teaspoon)
  salt
pepper

pink food colouring
8 rounded tablespoons
   white breadcrumbs
Second layer:
   1 425-g (15-oz) can
      mackerel in brine
   30 ml (2 tablespoons)
      lemon juice
   5 ml (1 level teaspoon)
      salt
   pepper
   100 g (4 oz) butter, melted
   5 rounded tablespoons
      white breadcrumbs
Place the salmon, ketchup, lemon juice, cream cheese, salt, a shake of pepper and a few drops of pink colouring in a liquidizer. Liquidize until the mixture is smooth. Pour into a basin, add the bread-crumbs, then press into con-

tainers; chill. Repeat this method with the ingredients for the second layer and spread the mixture on top.

To serve at once Chill, invert on a serving dish, garnish with fresh prawns, lemon and cucumber.

To freeze Cover, label and store for up to 4 months.

To use Turn out on to a serving dish and thaw in the refrigerator overnight or at room temperature.

SAVOURY QUICHES

Freeze quiches cooked or uncooked. Use 3·5-cm (1½-in)-deep tins or foil dishes. *Makes 2 20-cm (8-in) flans, 4 15-cm (6-in) flans or 12 individual flans*

▲ Vol-au-vents, smoked mackerel pâté (centre) and ratatouille.

Shortcrust pastry made from:
   300 g (¾ lb) plain flour
   75 g (3 oz) lard
   75 g (3 oz) margarine
   5 ml (1 level teaspoon)
      salt and water to mix
Base filling:
   4 eggs
   250 ml (½ pint) thin
      cream, evaporated milk
      or milk
   2·5 ml (½ level teaspoon)
      salt
   pepper
   100 g (4 oz) Cheddar
      cheese
Flavouring for filling:
   250 g (½ lb) streaky bacon

49

Line the flan dishes with pastry, turning the edges under to thicken, and flute with the fingers. Beat the eggs in a jug, add cream or milk, salt and a shake of pepper. Grate the cheese and sprinkle over the pastry bases. Remove rind and bone from bacon. Cut up bacon and divide between flans. Divide egg mixture between flans.

To freeze Cover with a labelled piece of foil (include cooking directions on label). Chill then freeze.

To serve at once Place on a baking sheet in the centre of a moderately hot oven (200°C, 400°F/Gas 6) for 20-40 minutes until pastry is golden and filling is almost set in centre.

To freeze cooked Cool, chill, cover with a labelled piece of foil.

To thaw Place on a baking sheet and heat in a moderate oven (190°C, 375°F/Gas 5) for 30-35 minutes. Or thaw at room temperature for about 4 hours.

Variations
For these, replace the bacon flavouring as directed below.

Washington quiche (see p. 76) Drain a large 396-g (14-oz) can of sweet corn with red and green peppers and divide between the flan cases.

Asparagus quiche Drain a large 396-g (14-oz) can of asparagus spears and divide between the flan cases. Use cream for the base.

Kipper quiche Cook two 278-g (10-oz) packets of frozen kipper fillets as directed on the packs. Pour off the liquid, flake the fish and divide between the cases.

Creamy haddock quiche Cook one 278-g (10-oz) packet of frozen haddock as directed on the pack. Drain, flake fish and mix with 250 g (8 oz) cottage cheese. Divide between the flan cases.

Cheese and onion quiche Replace Cheddar cheese with 200 g (8 oz) Gouda and divide between the flan cases. Fry ½ kg (1 lb) sliced onions; divide between the flan cases. Add 15 ml (1 level tablespoon) French mustard.

OTHER STARTERS
Cheese roulade
½ a Camembert cheese
250 g (8 oz) Gouda cheese
250 g (8 oz) medium-fat soft curd cheese
15 ml (1 level tablespoon) French mustard
15 ml (1 level tablespoon) paprika
30 ml (2 level tablespoons) chopped gherkins
30 ml (2 tablespoons) milk

Coating:
walnuts or salted peanuts
stuffed olives

Press the Camembert through a sieve into a bowl. Grate the Gouda finely and add to the bowl with the remaining ingredients; beat well. Form into a 20-cm (8-in) roll on a piece of foil. Roll up. Leave in a warm kitchen for one day for flavour to develop.

To use straight away Chill, then unwrap and roll in nuts and garnish with sliced stuffed olives. Place on a serving dish.

To freeze Chill, label and freeze. Store for up to 3 months. Thaw slowly in the refrigerator when required.

Ratatouille
2 large onions
3 tablespoons oil
1 clove garlic, crushed
2 large green peppers, sliced
2 large red peppers, sliced
1 kg (2 lb) tomatoes
½ kg (1 lb) courgettes, sliced
salt and pepper

Peel and chop the onions, place in a large saucepan with the oil and cook until golden brown. Add the garlic and sliced peppers. Skin and quarter the tomatoes; add to the pan. Add the courgettes, cover and cook over a low heat, stirring occasionally, until the vegetables are tender — about ¾ hour. Boil uncovered if mixture is too liquid.

To serve Chill and serve as a starter.

To freeze Pack in rigid containers. Remove and overwrap when frozen if desired. Store for up to 9 months.

Main-meal dishes

It is a great convenience to have a selection of dishes in the freezer for everyday use and entertaining. Ideally, it should be possible to re-heat or cook some of them from frozen so that a meal can be produced quickly. Joints of meat are best thawed slowly before cooking. Cook some bulk packs of meat in quantity. Often the best economies can be made by buying a huge turkey or chicken, cutting it into joints, then cooking the joints in different ways. If you make a habit of cooking double the usual quantity, eating half and freezing the rest, it won't feel like extra work.

Framed meat loaf

Make double quantities, half to serve hot, half to freeze.

1 large potato
1 large onion
100 g (4 oz) pig's kidney
200 g (½ lb) belly pork
500 g (1 lb) minced beef
4 slices bread
15 ml (1 level tablespoon) French mustard
30 ml (1 rounded tablespoon) tomato ketchup
10 ml (1 rounded teaspoon) salt
2 eggs
½ kg (1 lb) potatoes, cooked and mashed

Grate the raw potato and onion into a bowl. Mince or chop the kidney and pork. Add to the bowl with the beef. Make the bread into crumbs and add with the mustard, ketchup, salt and eggs. Mix well and press into 2 small loaf tins. Cover with foil and bake in a moderate oven (190°C, 375°F/Gas 5) for 1 hour. Turn out on to a serving plate, cover with mashed potato, mark with a fork, brush with egg or milk and bake in a hot oven (210°C, 425°F/Gas 7) until golden brown. Serve hot or cold in slices.

To freeze Turn the loaf out of the tin, cool then chill. Cover with potato, mark with a fork, then open-freeze until potato is firm. Wrap in foil, label, freeze and store for up to 4 months.

To use Brush with egg and

bake in a moderate oven for 1 hour.

Honey roast lamb

A boned, stuffed best-end-of-neck joint of lamb makes a compact joint for storing. Roast it whole and baste with honey. For a dinner party, tie the joint and cut into six noisettes before roasting.

Serves 6

1 small onion
1 small apple
knob of butter
2·5 ml (½ level teaspoon) cinnamon
50 g (2 oz) seedless raisins
1 slice bread from a small loaf
¾ kg (1 lb 12 oz) best-end-of-neck joint of lamb
salt and pepper
mustard
1 small orange
30 ml (2 level tablespoons) honey
watercress

Stuffing Peel and finely chop the onion and apple. Cook in butter in a small saucepan until soft but not browned. Stir in the cinnamon. Chop the raisins, cut the bread into small cubes or make crumbs, add to the saucepan and mix well. Bone the lamb (see p. 28), season with some salt and pepper then spread lightly with mustard. Spread the stuffing over and roll up. Tie with a butcher's slip knot (see p. 29) in 3 places if cooking in a piece, in 6 places for noisettes.

To use at once Cook the joint in a moderate oven (190°C, 375°F/Gas 5) for $\frac{1}{2}$ hour. Squeeze juice from the orange, reserving its shell. Mix the orange juice with honey, pour over the joint, then cook for a further $\frac{1}{2}$ hour, basting occasionally. Fill the orange shells with watercress to garnish. Cook the noisettes in a roasting tin for $\frac{1}{2}$ hour or in a grill pan without the rack for $\frac{1}{4}$ hour.

To freeze For noisettes, cut between the string and inter-leave with paper, wrap in foil, label, chill and freeze.

To use Thaw the joint com-pletely overnight in the re-frigerator or at room temp-erature for a few hours. Cook as above. Noisettes may be cooked from frozen. Roast for 45 minutes, grill for 25 minutes.

Chicken in ale

Thaw some frozen birds and make this recipe in quantity. It is quite safe to freeze the cooked dish (unlike re-freezing a raw bird, this is not dangerous). To feed a crowd, use a small turkey.

1 chicken, about 2 kg (4 lb) drawn weight
10 ml (1 rounded teaspoon) mixed dried herbs
30 ml (2 tablespoons) oil

25 g (1 oz) butter
4 rashers bacon
2 onions
1 clove garlic (optional)
45 ml (3 level tablespoons) plain flour
5 ml (1 level teaspoon) cinnamon
1 small (64-g, 2$\frac{1}{2}$-oz) can tomato purée
10 ml (1 rounded teaspoon) sugar
250 ml ($\frac{1}{2}$ pint) pale ale
salt and pepper

Place the chicken giblets in a saucepan. Cover with water and add the mixed dried herbs; cook for $\frac{3}{4}$ hour then strain and reserve the stock. Heat the oil and butter in a large frying-pan, fry the chicken to brown the breast then the thighs, and place in a large casserole. Remove the rind from the bacon, cut the bacon into strips. Peel the onions and garlic, if used, and cut the onion into quarters. Crush the garlic. Fry the bacon, onion and garlic until browned, stir in the flour and cinnamon. Add the tomato purée and sugar, then gradually add the pale ale followed by 250 ml ($\frac{1}{2}$ pint) giblet stock. Bring to the boil, stirring. Add salt and pepper to taste. Pour over the chicken in the casserole, cover and cook in a moderate oven (190°C, 375°F/Gas 5) for about 1 hour until the chicken is tender. Test by piercing the thigh joint with a skewer; the juices should be clear. Taste and add more season-ings if necessary.

To freeze Cut portions of chicken and freeze in con-tainers with some of the

sauce or pack the whole chicken in cling wrap. Pour the sauce into a freezer bag or boilable bag, exclude the air, seal, label and freeze separately. Pack together in a freezer bag. Store for up to 4 months.

To use Place in a casserole and heat gently for about 1 hour in a moderate oven or thaw and heat in a large saucepan.

Tartare beef casserole

Thawed, pre-packed minced beef can make a substantial meal. For top flavour, use a special mustard like Moutarde de Meaux or German mustard in the sauce. For a party dish, replace the mince with a mixture of minced veal and ham.

Serves 4

1 cup long-grain rice
1 onion extract cube
2·5 ml ($\frac{1}{2}$ level teaspoon) mixed dried herbs
90 ml (3 rounded tablespoons) chopped pickled cucumber, gherkin or piccalilli
6 stuffed olives (optional)
300 g (12 oz) minced beef
salt and pepper
Sauce:
    25 g (1 oz) margarine
    30 ml (2 level tablespoons) plain flour
    30 ml (3 rounded teaspoons) made mustard
    50 g (2 oz) Cheddar cheese, grated
    250 ml ($\frac{1}{2}$ pint) milk
    1 egg, beaten

Pre-heat a moderate oven (190°C, 375°F/Gas 5). Place

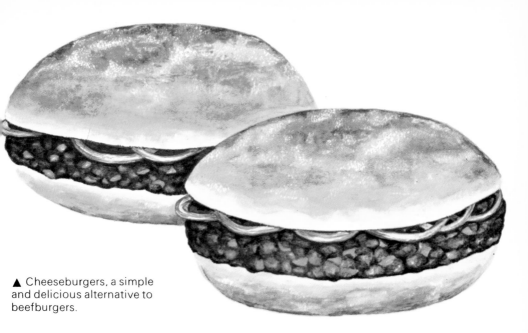

▲ Cheeseburgers, a simple and delicious alternative to beefburgers.

the rice in a saucepan. Make a cupful of stock with the cube and add it to the rice with the herbs and half a cup of water. Bring to the boil, cover the pan and cook over a very low heat for 15 minutes. Stir in the pickles and olives, if used. Mix the meat with a generous shake of salt and pepper; beat in half a cup of water. Spread half the rice over the base of a 1½-litre (3-pint) casserole. Cover with half the meat then repeat. Place all sauce ingredients except the egg in a saucepan. Whisk over a medium heat until the sauce has boiled. Remove from the heat and whisk in the egg, a little at a time. Add salt and pepper to taste. Pour over the meat, cover with a lid and cook for 15 minutes; remove the lid and cook for a

further ½-¾ hour until golden brown. Garnish with extra gherkins and stuffed olives, if desired.

To freeze Make the dish in foil containers or line the casserole with foil and remove after freezing. Freeze uncooked if mince has not been pre-frozen.

To use Partially thaw then increase cooking time under cover by ½ hour. Heat for ¾ hour in a moderate oven if cooked

Beefburgers
Makes 8
1 lb minced beef
10 ml (1 rounded teaspoon) salt
pepper
1 slice bread from a large loaf
milk
1 egg

1 small onion (optional)

Mix minced beef, salt and pepper together. Soak bread in 60 ml (4 tablespoons) milk, and beat into mince with egg. Finely grate the onion, if used, and mix in. Divide into 8 pieces and shape each into a flat cake on a floured board.

To freeze Interleave with plastic tissue then wrap in foil. Label, chill and freeze.

To use Grill or fry from frozen for 15 minutes.

Cheeseburgers
Make as above, but add 100 g (4 oz) grated, strongly-flavoured cheese.

Boned stuffed chicken
a fresh chicken, about 2 kg (4 lb) drawn weight
Stuffing:
75 g (3 oz) fat bacon

100 g (4 oz) lamb or
   chicken liver
250 g ($\frac{1}{2}$ lb) pork
   sausagemeat
25 g (1 oz) fresh
   breadcrumbs
salt and pepper
30 ml (1 rounded
   tablespoon) chopped
   parsley
25 g (1 oz) butter

Reserve the chicken liver from the giblets and place the remainder in a saucepan. To bone the chicken, see below.

Stuffing Chop the bacon and liver with the liver reserved from the giblets. Fry the bacon until fat runs, then add the liver and cook for 5 minutes. Mix the sausagemeat with the breadcrumbs, some salt and pepper and chopped parsley, add the contents of the frying-pan and mix well. To stuff the chicken, see below. Heat the butter in a roasting tin, place the chicken in it, breast side uppermost, and baste with butter. Roast in a moderately hot oven (200°C, 400°F/Gas 6) for 1 hour. Serve hot with vegetables or cold with salad.

To freeze Freeze uncooked, or cool, wrap in cling wrap, place in a freezer bag, label, chill and freeze. Store for up to 2 months.

To use Thaw overnight in refrigerator. Roast as above if serving hot.

Stuffing for a boned turkey

For a 5-kg (11-lb) oven-ready turkey, use double quantities as for chicken, but replace the sausagemeat with liver sausage. Place half the stuffing over the turkey, place 250 g ($\frac{1}{2}$ lb) pork sausagemeat in a roll down the centre, then spread the remaining liver-sausage stuffing over to enclose the sausagemeat. Sew the turkey skin together as shown below.

Basic beef stew

Save time by bulk-cooking this meat mixture and using it to make various meat dishes. Under-cook it slightly to allow for cooking the second time around.

2 kg (4 lb) stewing beef
250 g ($\frac{1}{2}$ lb) ox kidney
50 g (2 oz) cornflour
10 ml (2 level teaspoons)
   salt
5 ml (1 level teaspoon)
   pepper
$\frac{1}{2}$ kg (1 lb) onions
250 g ($\frac{1}{2}$ lb) carrots
4 sticks celery
50 g (2 oz) lard
1 litre (2 pints) beef stock
gravy browning (optional)

Remove the fat and gristle from the meat, and cut the meat into cubes. Cut the kidney into small pieces. Mix the cornflour, salt and

---

BONING AND STUFFING A CHICKEN

1. Cut off the tail and wing tips, cut through the bottom joint of each leg. Place the chicken breast-down and cut the skin along its back.

2. Gently cut away the flesh from the bone down to each wing, then to each leg; dislocate the joints, then remove the bones and continue cutting down the next bones.

3. Remove the wing and leg bones and turn the wings and legs inside out.

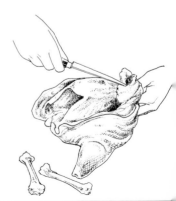

pepper in a bowl, add the meat and kidney and turn to coat. Peel and slice the onion, carrot and celery. Melt the lard in a large saucepan and fry the vegetables until golden brown. Remove from the pan and add the meat. Fry, stirring occasionally, until browned. Stir in any remaining seasoned cornflour, then return the vegetables to the pan. Stir in the stock gradually, then bring to the boil. Cover, reduce the heat and simmer until the meat is tender, (about $1\frac{1}{2}$ hours). Alternatively, either pressure-cook at high (15-lb) pressure for $\frac{1}{2}$ hour, reducing the stock to $\frac{3}{4}$ litre ($1\frac{1}{2}$ pints); or cook in a cool oven (150°C, 300°F/Gas 2) for $1\frac{1}{2}$ hours. Stir in some gravy browning. Pack in boilable bags or make preformed blocks. Use to make the following dishes.

Beefsteak pie Fill a foil pie-dish, cover with short-crust or puff pastry (there is no harm in using frozen pastry if it is being thawed and re-frozen quickly). Decorate the pie with pastry "leaves" but do not make a hole in the centre or brush with egg or milk. Cover, label, chill and freeze. Store for up to 3 months. To cook, place on a baking sheet in a cold oven, set heat to moderately hot (200°C, 400°F/Gas 6) and cook for about 1 hour, depending on depth.

High-hat stew Thaw the meat, bring to the boil and place a round of suet pastry on top. Cover and cook in a casserole for $\frac{1}{2}$ hour or in a saucepan for 20 minutes.

Beef cobbler Fill foil pie-dishes with meat mixture, and top with scone rounds. Sprinkle with grated cheese then cover, label and freeze. Bake as for beefsteak pie.

Beef vol-au-vent Roll out puff pastry to 1 cm ($\frac{1}{2}$ in) thick and cut into an oval. Cut half way through pastry 2·5 cm (1 in) from edge to form a rim. Brush with beaten egg and bake in a hot oven (210°C, 425°F/Gas 7) until risen and golden brown. Remove the centre, pull out any soft pastry and return to the oven for 5 minutes to crispen. Fill with basic beef (see above) and top with the pastry lid.

Homemade sausages

For these sausages, make a small quantity at first, until you know what level of seasonings and flavourings suits you best.

1 kg (2 lb) belly pork
4 slices bread
90 ml (6 tablespoons) milk
salt and pepper
fresh or dried sage and
    marjoram
ground coriander

4. When the meat is just attached to the carcass at the breast bone, cut away carefully, taking care not to break the skin.

5. Place the chicken skin side down and spread the stuffing down the centre.

6. Fold the chicken over to enclose the stuffing, then sew the skin at each side together with thick cotton. Leave a length of cotton at each end.

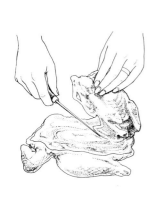

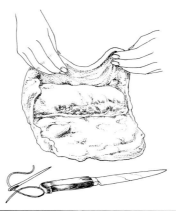

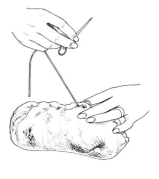

Remove the skin and bones from the meat, cut into strips, then mince coarsely. Break the bread into pieces, put one slice through the mincer and the remainder in a basin with 30 ml (2 tablespoons) milk. Leave to soak, beat with a fork, then add to the meat with 15 ml (1 level tablespoon) chopped fresh sage and marjoram or 5 ml (1 level teaspoon) dried herbs. Add 2·5-5 ml ($\frac{1}{2}$-1 level teaspoon) ground coriander. Mix well, then form into sausage shapes on a board coated with crisp, browned breadcrumbs. Or form into rounds with the hands, or in a burger press.

To freeze Open-freeze on a baking sheet for 1 hour, then wrap. Store for 2 months.

To use Fry or grill from frozen or thaw and use for stuffing poultry or lamb.

Java pork
Serves 4
2 medium-sized onions
1 stick celery
1 strip orange peel
butter
4 sparerib pork chops or
  steaks
5 ml (1 level teaspoon)
  curry powder
15 ml (1 level tablespoon)
  cornflour
1 chicken stock cube
30 ml (2 tablespoons)
  lemon juice
30 ml (2 tablespoons) thin
  cream

Peel and slice the onions. Wash and slice the celery. Chop the orange peel. Melt the butter in a large frying-pan, quickly brown the chops, then remove from the

pan. Fry the onion, celery, orange peel and curry powder until the onion is golden brown. Add the cornflour and a stock cube dissolved in 250 ml ($\frac{1}{2}$ pint) of boiling water. Stir in 125 ml ($\frac{1}{4}$ pint) of milk, bring to the boil, replace the meat, cover and simmer until the meat is tender (about $\frac{1}{2}$ hour). Taste and add salt and pepper if necessary, then stir in the lemon juice and cream. Serve with ribbon noodles.

To freeze Arrange the meat in a foil dish, cover with sauce and add a lid. Label, chill and freeze. Store for up to 2 months.

To use Thaw in the refrigerator or at room temperature. Loosen the lid and heat in a moderate oven for $\frac{1}{2}$ hour. Heat from frozen for about 50 minutes.

Chicken stroganoff
For a quick, special-occasion meal this has no equal. Try it also with turkey.
Serves 4
4 breasts chicken
30 ml (1 rounded
  tablespoon) plain flour
8 shallots
salt and pepper
50 g (2 oz) butter
100 g (4 oz) button
  mushrooms
125 ml ($\frac{1}{4}$ pint) white wine
  or chicken stock
125 ml ($\frac{1}{4}$ pint) soured
  cream
chopped parsley

Remove the skin and bone from the chicken (use to make stock). Cut the chicken into thin strips. Mix the flour with 5 ml (1 level teaspoon) salt and a gener-

ous shake of pepper. Coat the chicken in flour. Peel and slice the shallots. Melt the butter in a large frying-pan and fry the shallots for 2 minutes. Add the chicken and fry for about 7 minutes, stirring occasionally, until the chicken is golden brown. Wash the mushrooms, add to the pan and cook for 2 minutes. Immediately before serving, stir in the wine and boil rapidly to reduce by half. Remove from the heat and stir in the soured cream. Heat gently, but do not boil. Sprinkle with chopped parsley and serve at once with ribbon noodles or rice.

Turkey roll
The breast of a jointed turkey makes an economical roast for serving hot or cold. To vary, use sausage-meat instead of the pork mixture.
Serves 8
turkey breast meat
salt and pepper
250 g ($\frac{1}{2}$ lb) salt or fresh
  belly of pork
2 slices bread
2·5 ml ($\frac{1}{2}$ level teaspoon)
dried thyme

Heat the oven to 200°C, 400°F/Gas 6. Sprinkle the turkey with some salt and pepper. Remove the bones and skin, then mince the pork and bread. Mix in the thyme and some salt and pepper. Spread over the underside of the breast meat, roll up, then roast in a covered casserole for 1 hour. Make the gravy with the

▶ Pictured here are stuffed onions, Java pork and homemade sausages.

juices from the casserole and serve hot with roast potatoes and vegetables or cold with salad.

Basic minced beef

A store of cooked mince can be used for a variety of dishes that will store in the freezer for up to 3 months.

Serves 12

1½ kg (3 lb) minced beef
250 g (½ lb) lamb's liver
½ kg (1 lb) onions
25 g (1 oz) lard
125-g (5-oz) can tomato purée
10 ml (1 rounded teaspoon) mixed dried herbs
3 beef stock cubes
50 g (2 oz) cornflour
salt and pepper

Peel and chop the onion. Place the liver in a large saucepan with lard and fry lightly until just firm. Remove from the pan and chop finely. Place the beef and onion in the pan; fry over a low heat until the onion is browned. Stir in the tomato purée, herbs and liver. Dissolve the stock cubes in 1 litre (1½ pints) of boiling water, add to the pan, cover and simmer for 1 hour. Blend the cornflour with a little water, add some salt and pepper, and gravy browning and stir into the meat mixture. Taste and add more salt and pepper if necessary.

To freeze As for basic beef casserole.

Use for these dishes:

Shepherd's pie Place in foil pie-dishes and top with creamed potato.

Spaghetti bolognese Serve with spaghetti and top

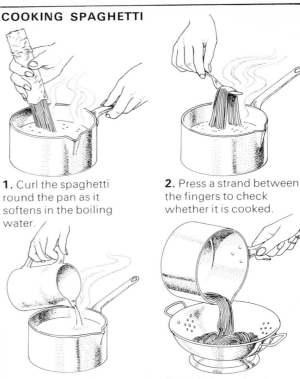

COOKING SPAGHETTI

1. Curl the spaghetti round the pan as it softens in the boiling water.

2. Press a strand between the fingers to check whether it is cooked.

3. Add some cold water to stop the cooking.

4. Drain in a colander. Return to the pan with a knob of butter.

with Parmesan cheese.

Minced beef pie Make as for beefsteak pie. Add cooked root vegetables, butter beans or baked beans in tomato to meat, if desired. Thicken with some grated potato for a two-crust plate pie.

Lasagne (for 4) Par-boil sheets of lasagne (250 g, ½ lb), drain and spread a layer in a shallow oblong ovenproof dish, then half the minced beef (one-third the recipe quantity), then a layer of savoury white sauce made with ½ litre (1 pint) of

milk. Repeat the layers and top with grated Parmesan cheese. Cover with foil, label, chill and freeze.

To use, remove cover, dot with butter and heat from frozen in a moderate oven (190°C, 375°F/Gas 5) for about 1 hour.

Stuffed onions Par-boil large onions for ½ hour, remove the centres, chop and add to mince with a little lightly fried bacon. Place in a roasting tin, baste with bacon fat and bake until the onions are tender — about ¾ hour.

Puddings and desserts

It is best to freeze the most perishable desserts, such as mousses and creams. Cheesecakes are ideal for storing. If they are made in large quantities and the surplus is frozen, the flavour will actually improve in the freezer. Pastry bakes well from frozen; to have a selection of fruit pies in store is a great convenience.

Fruit mousse

Use fresh, canned or frozen fruit purée and a jelly of a complementary flavour.

1 jelly tablet
boiling water (or fruit syrup from can)
125 ml ($\frac{1}{4}$ pint) sweetened fruit purée
125 ml ($\frac{1}{4}$ pint) double cream or evaporated milk
lemon juice (optional)
food colouring (optional)

Place the jelly in a measuring jug and make up to 250 ml ($\frac{1}{2}$ pint) with boiling water or syrup; stir until dissolved and leave until beginning to set. Whisk the evaporated milk or cream until thick, then whisk in the fruit purée, followed by the partially set jelly. Whisk in the lemon juice and food colouring, if the flavour and colour require them. Pour into plastic dessert dishes, individual

jelly moulds or a $\frac{3}{4}$ litre (1$\frac{1}{2}$-pint) jelly mould. Cover, label, chill and freeze. Store for up to 3 months.

To use Thaw at room temperature for 1$\frac{1}{2}$ hours or for 5 hours in the refrigerator. Serve with extra fruit purée, fruit or cream.

Chilled citrus cheesecake

This soufflé mixture is useful for large-scale entertaining as it cuts well into sixteen portions.

Serves 6

150 g (6 oz) digestive biscuits
5 ml (1 level teaspoon) cinnamon
50 g (2 oz) butter
30 ml (2 level tablespoons) golden syrup

Topping:

1 envelope (15 ml or 1 level tablespoon) gelatine
2 eggs
1 lemon
1 medium-sized orange
100 g (4 oz) sugar
325 g ($\frac{3}{4}$ lb) cottage, cream or curd cheese
125 ml ($\frac{1}{4}$ pint) double cream

Crush the biscuits (see above) and mix with the cinnamon, melted butter and syrup. Spread in a 20-cm (8-in) loose-based cake tin; press with the back of a spoon.

To make topping Place 3 tablespoons water in a cup and sprinkle the gelatine on top. Separate the eggs; place the yolks and whites in separate bowls. Scrub the lemon and orange, cut one slice of orange from the centre and two slices of lemon and reserve for decoration. Grate the rinds into the bowl with the egg yolks, then squeeze the juice and add to the bowl. Add the sugar, then place the bowl over a saucepan of boiling water and whisk until the mixture is thick; whisk in the softened gelatine and remove the bowl from the heat. Sieve the cottage cheese and whisk into the mixture in the bowl. Whisk the cream until just thick, whisk the egg whites until stiff but not dry, and fold into the mixture using a metal spoon.

Pour into the tin and leave to set in the refrigerator. Remove the side of the tin by placing the base on a smaller tin and pulling the side down. Decorate with orange and lemon slices.

To freeze Open-freeze, un-decorated, on the base. Remove the base and wrap in foil when firm; seal, label and store for up to 3 months. **To thaw** Leave in the refrigerator overnight or thaw for 6 hours at room temperature

Battenberg charlotte
Makes 8 portions
1 battenberg cake
1 small (234-g, $8\frac{1}{2}$-oz) can fruit cocktail
1 lemon jelly
1 small can evaporated milk
whipped cream

Line a 1-litre (1-lb) loaf tin with freezer paper or foil. Cut the cake into 8 slices and arrange around the sides of the tin, cutting to fit if necessary. Drain the syrup from a can of fruit into a saucepan, add the jelly and heat gently until the jelly has dissolved; pour into a measuring jug and make up to 250 ml ($\frac{1}{2}$ pint) with cold water. Place 30 ml (2 tablespoons) jelly in a saucer and stir in 30 ml (2 tablespoons) water. Dip one side of each piece of cake into the jelly and press against the side of the tin. Arrange pieces of fruit with a cherry in the centre on the base of the tin; pour in the remaining jelly from the saucer and place in the refrigerator to set. Whisk the evaporated milk until thick. Add 30 ml (2 tablespoons) water to the jelly in the jug then whisk into the milk. Fold in the

fruit cocktail then pour into the tin; leave in the refrigerator until set

To use Invert on a serving dish, remove the paper or foil and decorate with cream and pieces of cherry and angelica around the base.

To freeze Place in the freezer, remove from the tin and over-wrap with more foil or paper. Store for up to 2 months. Unwrap and thaw on a serving dish

Janne's pavlova
By popular request, a friend called Janne would arrive at parties in New Zealand with this soft-textured pavlova. It will not keep in a tin and it is best frozen.
3 egg whites
5 ml (1 teaspoon) vinegar
100 g (7 oz) castor sugar
125 ml ($\frac{1}{4}$ pint) whipped cream
fresh, frozen or canned fruit
Prepare a moderately hot oven (200°C, 400°F/Gas 6). Line the base and side of a 20-cm (8-in) cake tin. Whisk the egg whites until stiff (make sure there is no egg yolk included and that neither bowl nor whisk are at all greasy). Whisk in the vinegar then add the sugar gradually, whisking all the time. Spread in the tin, place in the centre of the oven and turn heat down to cool (100°C, 200°F/Gas $\frac{1}{4}$). Cook for $\frac{1}{2}$ hour then turn off the oven and leave the pavlova there until cold.
To serve at once Invert on to a serving plate, whip the cream and spread over; decorate with fruit.
To freeze Invert on a piece of foil, remove the paper,

wrap, label and freeze. Store for up to 4 months.
To thaw Unwrap, place the frozen pavlova on a serving plate, thaw for 3 hours at room temperature then decorate with cream and fruit

Strawberry almond cream
Serves 6
This is one of the quickest and most delicious of dinner-party desserts. Meringues can be substituted for the macaroons for a sweeter flavour. A tangy fruit, such as raspberries, is best for the sauce if using meringues.
75 g (3 oz) almond macaroons
butter
200 ml (7 fluid ounces) double cream
30 ml (3 rounded teaspoons) castor sugar
125 ml (5 fluid ounces) soured cream
250 ml ($\frac{1}{2}$ pint) sweetened strawberry purée
10 ml (2 teaspoons) lemon juice
Crush one macaroon finely and cut up the remainder. Butter a $\frac{1}{2}$-litre (1-pint) metal jelly mould, bombe mould or 15-cm (6-in) cake tin. Place the crushed macaroon in the mould or tin and turn to coat all over. Whisk

▶ Foamy desserts, such as these gooseberry and blackcurrant mousses, store well in the freezer. Also shown are chilled citrus cheesecake, battenberg charlotte and strawberry almond cream with strawberry purée.

⚠ Folding in crushed macaroons.

the double cream and sugar together until thick. Whisk in the soured cream, then fold in the chopped macaroons. Spread in the tin, cover with foil, label and freeze. Store for up to 2 months.

To use Place the tin in the frozen food compartment of the refrigerator for 1 hour before serving. Mix the strawberry purée and lemon juice and pour into a jug. Quickly dip the tin in hot water and invert the cream on to a serving plate.

Fruit pies

Make two pie crusts on ovenproof enamel or foil plates in the usual way. Or make up the components of the pies to save freezer space.

Filling Make this when the fruit is in season. Fruits that discolour, such as apples, need blanching. Otherwise, cook the filling slightly. Make a syrup with sugar and water, add the apples, cover and cook on full heat for a

few minutes. Mix in some blackberries, black currants, raspberries, strawberries or sultanas and spice. Moist fruits such as plums and soft fruits need mixing with corn-flour or potato flour to hold the juice and prevent the pastry becoming wet. Mix it with sugar then fold into the fruit to coat. Use 15 ml (1 level tablespoon) cornflour or potato flour and 60-90 ml (2-3 rounded tablespoons) sugar to each $\frac{1}{2}$ kg (1 lb) fruit.

To freeze Line a plate with foil or cling wrap, allowing sufficient to over-wrap the filling. Spread the filling to within 1·5 cm ($\frac{1}{2}$ in) of the edge. Enclose in the wrapping, press out the air, chill, label and freeze.

Pastry Make shortcrust pastry and roll out thinly to 1·5 cm ($\frac{1}{2}$ in) bigger than the plates. Interleave with sheets of foil and freeze.

To make pies Remove the pastry sheets and leave to thaw until pliable—about 20 minutes. Make pies using a frozen block of pie filling. Brush with water, sprinkle with sugar and make a hole in the centre.

To bake Place the pie on a baking sheet and place in the centre of the oven. Set the oven to moderate (190° C, 375°F/Gas 5) and bake for 55-60 minutes until the pastry is golden brown.

Freezer trifle

Traditional trifles of sponge cake, jelly and custard separate on freezing so the method must be adapted this way. Do not put your best

soaked sponge cake
custard
sweetened whipped cream topped with grated chocolate

trifle bowl in the freezer—it may crack.
Serves 4-5
4 trifle sponge cakes
strawberry jam
1 large orange
$\frac{1}{2}$ a lemon
2 bananas
1 (411-g, 14$\frac{1}{2}$-oz) can dairy custard
125 ml ($\frac{1}{4}$ pint) whipping or double cream
10 ml (1 rounded teaspoon) castor sugar
grated chocolate

Line an ovenproof or plastic dish of similar size to your trifle bowl with cling wrap. Cut the sponge cakes in halves and sandwich with jam. Cut into pieces and place in the bowl. Squeeze the juice from the orange and lemon; peel the bananas, sieve and mix into the juice. Pour over the sponge cakes to soak. Spread the custard over. Whip the cream and sugar until just thick; spread over the custard, then sprinkle with grated chocolate. Cover with cling wrap, then freeze. When firm, remove from the dish and wrap in foil or a freezer bag.

To use Remove the wrapping and place in the trifle bowl. Leave to thaw for about 6 hours at room temperature or overnight in the refrigerator.

Raspberry almond flan

Bake in a large (30-cm, 12-in) flan case for a party.

Pastry:
125 g (5 oz) butter
200 g (8 oz) self-raising flour
50 g (2 oz) castor sugar
1 egg

Filling:
100 g (4 oz) soft margarine
100 g (4 oz) castor sugar
100 g (4 oz) ground almonds
25 g (1 oz) ground rice
almond essence
2 eggs
2 trifle sponges
$\frac{1}{2}$ kg (1 lb) raspberries, peaches, apricots, pears or cherries (fresh, frozen or canned)
apricot jam
flaked browned almonds

Rub the butter into the flour, stir in 50 g (2 oz) sugar and bind with beaten egg. Knead well until smooth, then chill. Beat together the margarine, 100 g (4 oz) sugar, ground almonds and ground rice, a few drops of almond essence and the eggs. Roll out the pastry and line two 20-cm (8-in) flan tins; sprinkle the bases with crumbled sponge cake and arrange a layer of raspberries over each. Pour the almond mixture over and bake in a moderate oven (190°C, 375°F/Gas 5) for

about 35 minutes until golden brown.

To freeze Open-freeze on the flan-tin bases, then wrap in foil, label and store in the freezer for up to 3 months.

To use Thaw, then brush with warmed sieved jam and sprinkle with nuts. Serve with cream.

Fruit medley flan

A golden sponge topping complements both sweet and tart fruits when mixed in a flan.

shortcrust pastry made from
150 g (6 oz) flour
300 g (12 oz) prepared fruit (apples, pears canned or frozen peaches, apricots, raspberries)
1 egg
50 g (2 oz) castor sugar
vanilla essence
25 g (1 oz) self-raising flour
apricot jam
flaked almonds

Prepare a moderately hot oven (200°C, 400°F/Gas 6). Roll out the pastry and line a 20-cm (8-in) fluted flan ring; spread the fruit over the pastry. Whisk the egg and sugar together until thick, whisk in a few drops of vanilla essence then fold in

▲ Support the pastry on the rolling pin while lining the flan dish.

the flour; pour over the fruit and bake in the centre of the oven for $\frac{1}{2}$ hour. Remove the flan ring and bake for a further 5 minutes.

To serve at once Brush the surface with sieved apricot jam, then scatter with almonds. Serve warm or cold with cream or custard.

To freeze Omit the jam and almonds, wrap, label and chill. Store for up to 3 months.

To thaw Unwrap, place on a serving plate and leave to thaw at room temperature— about 4 hours. Decorate with jam and almonds. To serve hot, place on a baking sheet and heat in a moderate oven (180°C, 350°F/Gas 4) for about 40 minutes. Decorate with jam and almonds.

Rich baked cheesecake

This cheesecake has a pronounced rich soft-cheese flavour and texture. Freeze whole or in wedges.

Base:
100 g (4 oz) self-raising flour
50 g (2 oz) butter
50 g (2 oz) icing sugar
1 egg yolk

Topping:
75 g (3 oz) butter
50 g (2 oz) castor sugar
2·5 ml ($\frac{1}{2}$ teaspoon) vanilla essence
1 egg yolk
rind and juice of $\frac{1}{2}$ a lemon
25 g (1 oz) cornflour
$\frac{1}{2}$ kg (1 lb) medium-fat curd cheese
142 ml ($\frac{1}{4}$ pint) soured cream
50 g (2 oz) sultanas (optional)
2 egg whites

Prepare a moderate oven (180°C, 350°F/Gas 4).

To make base Place the flour in a bowl and rub in the butter. Stir in the icing sugar and egg yolk and mix to a firm dough; knead until smooth. Roll out and press over the base of a 20-cm (8-in) loose-based cake tin. Bake in the centre of the oven until golden brown (about 25 minutes).

To make topping Cream the butter and castor sugar together, beat in the vanilla essence, egg yolk, lemon rind and juice and cornflour, then the cheese, soured cream and sultanas, if used. Whisk the egg whites until just stiff, then fold into the cheese mixture, cutting through with a metal spoon. Spread over the base in the tin and bake on the centre shelf of the oven for 45 minutes. Leave to cool in the tin, remove, then chill overnight in the refrigerator. This cheesecake will store for a week in a refrigerator.

To freeze Loosen the edge, remove the side of cake tin by placing it on a smaller tin and pulling down. Freeze on the base until firm; remove, wrap in foil, label and return to the freezer.

To thaw Unwrap and place on a serving plate. Thaw overnight in the refrigerator or for 6 hours at room temperature. If required in a hurry, thaw for 1 hour then cut in wedges.

Quick cheesecake

This creamy basic cheesecake makes three 15-cm (6-in) or two 20-cm (8-in)

cheesecakes in foil pie plates. Decorate the top with fresh, frozen or canned fruit or whipped cream and chocolate curls.

Base:
  75 g (3 oz) butter
  150 g (6 oz) digestive biscuits
  75 g (3 oz) castor sugar

Cheesecake:
  1 lemon jelly
  100 g (4 oz) unsalted butter
  250 ml (8 fluid oz) milk
  2·5 ml ($\frac{1}{2}$ teaspoon) vanilla essence
  100 g (4 oz) low- or medium-fat cottage or curd cheese
  100 g (4 oz) full-fat cream cheese
  rind and juice of $\frac{1}{2}$ a small lemon
  142 ml ($\frac{1}{4}$ pint) soured cream

Topping:
  fresh, canned or frozen fruit or whipped cream
  cornflour, arrowroot or potato flour

To make base Melt the butter in a saucepan. Make crumbs with the biscuits in a liquidizer and add to the pan with sugar. Mix well, then press into the bases and up the sides of foil plates; chill.

To make cheesecake Cut up the jelly and place in a liquidizer. Place the butter and milk in a saucepan, bring to the boil, add to the goblet and liquidize until the mixture is smooth. Add the remaining cheesecake ingredients and liquidize until smooth. Place the liquidizer in the refrigerator and leave until the mixture is almost set. Scrape down the sides

with a spatula, replace the lid and liquidize until foamy. Divide between the plates then leave to set in the refrigerator. Add the topping before or after freezing.

To make topping Prepare the fruit, drain if necessary and thicken the syrup or juice with cornflour, arrowroot or potato flour (cornflour gives a cloudy glaze). Arrange the fruit on the cheesecake and glaze with thickened syrup. Alternatively, top with whipped cream and chocolate curls.

To freeze Cover with foil and label, if untopped; open-freeze before covering, if topped.

To thaw Unwrap, place on a serving plate and leave overnight in the refrigerator or thaw at room temperature for 4-6 hours.

Iced maraschino gâteau

Serves 6-8
Sponge:
  50 g (2 oz) castor sugar
  1 egg
  25 g (1 oz) self-raising flour
  25 g (1 oz) cornflour
Topping:
  50 g (2 oz) almond macaroons
  25 g (1 oz) plain chocolate
  12 scoops vanilla ice cream
  1 small (113-g, 4-oz) jar maraschino cherries
  125 ml ($\frac{1}{4}$ pint) double cream
  10 ml (1 rounded teaspoon) sugar

Prepare a hot oven (200°C, 400°F/Gas 6). Line the base of a round 20-cm (8-in) loose-based cake tin with greaseproof paper. Whisk the sugar and egg until thick, sift the flour and cornflour together and fold into the egg mixture. Pour into the tin and bake in the centre of the oven for about 20 minutes until golden brown. Remove the tin, remove the paper, cool, replace in the tin then chill. Break up the macaroons. Reserving two squares, chop the chocolate finely; place in a bowl with the ice cream. Reserving four cherries, add the remainder and the syrup from the bottle. Mix quickly until evenly blended, then spread over the sponge in the tin and freeze.

To use Place on a smaller tin and remove the side, then the base of the tin. Whisk the cream and sugar together and pipe 16 whirls around the edge. Cut the reserved cherries in halves and place a piece on each alternate whirl. Melt the chocolate, place in a greaseproof-paper piping bag, fold down the top, snip a small piece from the point and pipe fine lines over the remaining cream

▼ Piping chocolate over the cream whirls.

whirls. Keep in the freezer or frozen food compartment until ready to serve.

To freeze Leave on the base and open-freeze. Wrap the reserved cherries and chocolate in cling wrap. Remove the base, wrap in cling wrap or foil, label and store for up to 2 months. Pipe the cream into 16 whirls on some foil, open-freeze then pack in a freezer bag with the base and decoration.

To use Unwrap, place on a serving plate and place cream whirls around the edge. Decorate with cherries and chocolate.

Profiteroles
50 g (2 oz) margarine
75 g (2½ oz) plain flour
2 eggs
250 ml (½ pint) double cream
10 ml (1 rounded teaspoon) sugar
75 g (3 oz) plain chocolate
75 g (3 oz) golden syrup
Prepare a moderately hot oven (200°C, 400°F/Gas 6). Grease a baking sheet. Melt the margarine in a saucepan with 125 ml (¼ pint) of water, bring to the boil, re-

move from the heat and add the flour all at once. Beat with a wooden spoon until the mixture forms a ball and comes away from the side of the pan. Beat the eggs. Beat into the mixture a little at a time. Using a teaspoon, place the mixture on a baking sheet in about 30 heaps, or pipe with a large plain tube fitted into a nylon piping bag. Bake in the centre of the oven for 30-35 minutes until the buns are risen and golden. Split each one to allow steam to escape. Whip the cream with the sugar then fill the buns.

To make sauce Place the chocolate and syrup in a bowl over a saucepan of boiling water and stir until melted.

To serve Pile the choux buns on a serving dish and pour a little sauce over. Serve the rest separately.

To freeze Pile the filled buns in a freezer bag. Pack the sauce in a tub and freeze. Pack in a bag with the frozen buns.

To use Thaw the buns in the refrigerator; serve with chocolate sauce.

◄ Making chocolate sauce in a basin over boiling water, and adding golden syrup.

Ice cream parlour

In Roman times, slaves made regular trips to the mountains to bring back snow for their masters so that it could be used to chill the ingredients for some sort of 'ice cream'. Today, stocking up the freezer with bought or homemade ice cream is far simpler. This versatile food can be teamed up with sauces, fruits, chocolate and nuts or used to make sumptuous iced gâteaux.

Making perfect ice cream

Ice cream can have a base of cream or custard—the richer the mixture the smoother the ice cream. Skilful mixing can improve the texture of less rich, economy ice creams. Repeated stirring helps the formation of small ice crystals. This can be achieved easily with an ice-cream maker, which has paddles to whisk the mixture as it freezes. Some models are large-capacity hand-cranked ice buckets with paddle mechanisms; there are also small, electrically operated ice-cream makers that will fit into the freezer or the frozen food compartment of a refrigerator. Alternatively, the mixture can be half frozen in the freezer or

▲ A small electrically operated churn makes really smooth ice cream.

frozen food compartment of the refrigerator, whisked, then frozen until firm.

Storing ice cream

Use oblong plastic boxes for easy scooping and cover with a lid. Small containers are best. Store for up to 3 months at a steady temperature.

Serving ice cream

In order that the flavour and texture of the ice cream can be appreciated, it is important to serve it at the correct temperature. Place the container in the frozen food compartment of the refrigerator for at least an hour before serving. Use a scoop and shave off thin layers of ice cream which curl into the scoop. Keep the ice cream level in the container. Serve with crisp wafers or biscuits.

Ice lollies

Well designed lolly kits are available from most firms that supply freezer packaging. Make sure replacement sticks are available. Transfer lollies from the freezer to the frozen food compartment of the refrigerator for an hour or so before serving, otherwise they could cause freezer burn on the lips.

Fruit lollies Use sweetened

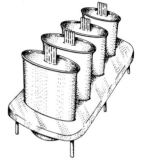

fruit purée or fruit cordial. Make up with 1 tablespoon (15 ml) to each 2 tablespoons (30 ml) water.

Cream ice lollies Use a custard-based ice cream (see p. 67).

Choc-ice lollies Chill the mould and line with melted chocolate (see choc ices). Fill with ice cream.

Rich ice cream

This ice cream has a soft, creamy texture. It does not need to be whisked after freezing. Flavour as below.

2 eggs
50 g (2 oz) icing sugar
5 ml (1 teaspoon) vanilla
 essence
125 ml ($\frac{1}{4}$ pint) double
 cream

Separate the eggs, placing the whites and yolks in separate bowls. Whisk the whites until stiff, then whisk in sifted icing sugar, a little at a time. Whisk the yolks with the vanilla essence then whisk into the whites. Whisk the cream until it stands in soft peaks, then fold into the egg mixture and mix gently until well blended. Place in an oblong plastic container (for easy scooping) and freeze.

Flavourings for rich ice cream

Chocolate Melt 75 g (3 oz) plain chocolate and beat into the yolk mixture.

Coffee Dissolve 10 ml (1 rounded teaspoon) instant coffee in 15 ml (1 tablespoon) boiling water. Beat into the yolk mixture. Add 30 ml (2 tablespoons) rum or coffee liqueur, if desired.

Ginger Add 30 ml (2 level tablespoons) chopped stem ginger; omit the vanilla.

Strawberry Add a purée made from 250 g ($\frac{1}{2}$ lb) strawberries to the egg yolks. Add a few drops of red food colouring and sugar to taste.

Raspberry Make as strawberry.

Orange Add 100 ml (4 fl oz) concentrated frozen orange juice, just thawed, to the egg yolk mixture; omit the vanilla

Tutti-frutti Add 25 g (1 oz) maraschino cherries, chopped, 15 ml (1 level tablespoon) chopped peel, 15 ml (1 level tablespoon) chopped angelica and a few drops of almond essence.

Mint Fold 50 g (2 oz) chopped mint chocolate cracknel into the mixture. Tint pale green.

Banana Mash 2 ripe bananas with 30 ml (2 tablespoons) lemon juice and add to egg yolk mixture.

▲ Scoop ice cream by drawing the scoop over the ice cream's surface. The ice cream will form a thin curl in the scoop.

Nut fudge Fold 25 g (1 oz) roasted chopped almonds and 25 g (1 oz) chopped bitter chocolate to vanilla or chocolate ice cream.

Vanilla ice cream

A custard base gives ice cream a full flavour. For grand occasions make an egg custard and use double cream. For economy, use a pouring custard made with custard powder, or canned custard, and replace the cream with whisked evaporated milk. Flavour as rich ice cream.

2 egg yolks
100 g (4 oz) castor sugar
10 ml (1 rounded teaspoon) custard powder
250 ml ($\frac{1}{2}$ pint) milk
5 ml (1 teaspoon) vanilla essence
125-250 ml ($\frac{1}{4}$-$\frac{1}{2}$ pint) double cream

Chill a bowl and a plastic container. Beat the yolks,

castor sugar and custard powder together in a basin. Heat the milk, beat into the egg yolk mixture, then return to the saucepan and cook over a low heat, stirring continuously until just boiling. Beat in the vanilla essence, then pour into a basin, cover with cling wrap to prevent a skin forming, leave to cool, then chill. Whisk the cream until it just holds its shape, then fold in the chilled custard. Pour into the plastic container, place in the freezer (or the frozen food compartment of a refrigerator) and leave for about 2 hours until a 2·5 cm (1 in) area round the edge is frozen. Scrape into a chilled bowl, whisk until smooth, then return to the container. Cover with a lid or foil and freeze until firm.

To serve Leave in the frozen food compartment of the refrigerator for 1 hour to soften slightly.

Choc ices (see p. 69)
milk or plain cooking chocolate
bought or homemade vanilla-flavoured ice cream or water ice
cream, fruit or chocolate to decorate

Select flexible plastic moulds such as yoghurt or cream pots, individual plastic dessert cups or lolly moulds. Rub the inside of each mould with cotton wool then chill in the refrigerator. Break up the chocolate and melt in a bowl over a saucepan of hot (not boiling) water. Take one mould out of the refrigerator at a time, place 2 tablespoons melted chocolate in the base, then turn gently to coat the side in chocolate. Pour the surplus back into a bowl and invert the mould on to a plate; leave to set, then chill. Fill with homemade ice cream when half frozen. To use bought ice cream, place scoops of ice cream in a bowl, add some flavouring (see below) if desired, mix gently until slightly soft then press into the mould; place in the freezer until firm—about 1 hour.

To serve at once Invert the mould on to a serving dish, gently press the base and pull out the side. Quickly decorate, then serve.

To store Cover with a lid or foil and label. Store for up to 2 months.

Flavourings for choc ices
Prepare and chill before lining the mould.

Rum and raisin Add dark rum to seedless raisins in a basin, cover and leave to plump up.

Tutti-frutti Add chopped sultanas, maraschino or glacé cherries, chopped angelica, broken walnuts and honey.

Crème de menthe Add mint liqueur or peppermint oil and tint pale green.

Caribbean coffee Add strong coffee and dark rum.

Orange sparkle Fill with orange water ice.

Water ices
Water ices or sorbets are simply fruit purée or juice mixed with sugar syrup and frozen.

Lemon water ice (basic method)
Dissolve 125 g (4 oz) sugar in 250 ml ($\frac{1}{2}$ pint) water. Bring to the boil and boil on full heat without stirring for 2 minutes. Cool and chill. Mix with 250 ml ($\frac{1}{2}$ pint) lemon juice and the finely grated rind of 1 lemon. Pour into a shallow metal tin and freeze until just firm. Turn into a chilled bowl and whisk until mushy. Whisk an egg white, if desired, until softly stiff, then fold into the lemon mixture, cutting through the mixture with a metal spoon to avoid breaking down the foam. Place in a plastic container, cover with a lid or foil and freeze until firm. Store for up to 6 months.

To use Place the container in the frozen food compartment of the refrigerator for at least one hour before serving to soften. Serve with crisp sugar biscuits.

Frozen lemons Cut tops off lemons and reserve, scoop out the flesh and press through a sieve to obtain the juice; make and fill with a water ice, as above.

Orange water ice Make as lemon water ice using 250 ml ($\frac{1}{2}$ pint) orange juice, the grated rind of 1 orange, sugar syrup and 45 ml (3 tablespoons) lemon juice.

Frozen oranges Fill orange shells with orange water ice.

Gooseberry water ice Use $\frac{1}{2}$ kg (1 lb) gooseberries, cook then press through a sieve to make 250 ml ($\frac{1}{2}$ pint) purée. Make as above adding sugar syrup. Use other fruit purées this way.

Ice cream bombes
The name refers to the bombe mould in which these special ice-cream puddings are traditionally made. A basin, jelly mould or cake tin can be used in place of a bombe mould.

To de-mould, invert on a chilled serving plate, wring out a cloth in hot water and wrap it around the mould. Shake to de-mould. Replace the bombe in the freezer for half an hour, then decorate if desired.

Brandied berry bombe
Makes 2 1-litre (1$\frac{1}{2}$-pint) bombes
2 egg yolks
75 g (3 oz) granulated sugar
250 ml ($\frac{1}{2}$ pint) milk
2·5 ml ($\frac{1}{2}$ teaspoon) vanilla essence
250 ml ($\frac{1}{2}$ pint) double cream
45 ml (3 tablespoons) brandy
250 g ($\frac{1}{2}$ lb) raspberries or loganberries
2 egg whites
100 g (4 oz) castor sugar
Turn the refrigerator to its coldest setting. Chill the basins or moulds in the freezer. Whisk the egg yolk and sugar together. Boil the milk, whisk into the yolks then return to the saucepan and cook, stirring, over a low heat until the mixture coats the back of the spoon; stir

▶ A sumptuous selection of ice creams: gooseberry and water melon water ices, cassata and peach melba bombes, rich ice cream with chocolate sauce and rum and raisin choc ice.

in the vanilla essence, then chill. Whisk the cream until it just holds its shape, then fold into the custard mixture. Pour into a metal tray and freeze. Leave for about 1 hour until partially frozen, place in a chilled bowl and whisk until smooth; whisk in the brandy. Pour into the chilled basins or moulds and leave in the freezer until half set—about $\frac{1}{2}$ hour.

Meanwhile, cook the raspberries or loganberries in 30 ml (2 tablespoons) water; press through a sieve and cool. Whisk the egg whites until stiff, whisk in the castor sugar then, gradually, the fruit purée. Pour into a metal tray and freeze until firm. Remove one basin or mould from the freezer, press the ice cream up the side with a metal spoon, leaving a hollow in the centre; smooth the ice cream then return the basin or mould to the freezer. Repeat with the other basin. When the side of each is firm, fill the centres with fruit mixture. Cover with foil and replace in the freezer.

▼ Pressing the outer layer of ice cream round the mould for a bombe.

To serve De-mould on to a serving plate (see above); decorate with piped whipped cream and some raspberries, if desired. Replace in the freezer or place in the frozen food compartment of the refrigerator.

To store De-mould on to a piece of foil, open-freeze for $\frac{1}{2}$ hour then over-wrap with foil. Store for up to 2 months.

Variations
Peach melba bombe (see p. 69) Make the outside layer by whisking sugar and egg yolks together over hot water until thick, whisk in 125 ml ($\frac{1}{4}$ pint) peach purée made from fresh or canned fruit, 30 ml (2 tablespoons) lemon juice and 250 ml ($\frac{1}{2}$ pint) cream. Fill with raspberry ice as above.

Coffee cream bombe Set the outside with brandy-flavoured ice cream. Fill the centre with coffee ice made by dissolving 30 ml (2 level tablespoons) instant coffee in 125 ml ($\frac{1}{4}$ pint) water; stir in 5 ml (1 level teaspoon) gelatine softened in 5 ml (1 teaspoon) cold water. Cool, then whisk into the egg whites and sugar.

Mocha bombe Add 50 g (2 oz) plain chocolate and 10 ml (2 level teaspoons) cocoa to milk. Replace the brandy with rum if desired. Fill the centre with coffee ice, as above. Mix in 25 g (1 oz) raisins if desired.

Chocolate orange bombe Make chocolate ice cream for the outside as above. Fill the centre with orange ice made by replacing the fruit purée with 125 ml ($\frac{1}{4}$ pint)

concentrated Florida orange juice.

Sunburst orange bombe Flavour the outside with rum or brandy and fill the centre with orange ice made as above. Add chopped plain chocolate to the orange ice, if desired.

St Clement's bombe Omit the brandy. Flavour the ice cream with the rind and juice of 2 lemons. Add some yellow food colouring. Fill the centre with orange ice made as for chocolate orange bombe.

Making bombes with prepared ice cream
Experiment with different flavours of homemade or bought ice cream or sorbets. Add concentrated flavourings and dried or crystallized fruits. To fill a 1-litre (2-pint) basin, use about $\frac{1}{2}$ litre (2 pint) for each layer.

Cassata (see p.69) Line a mould with chocolate ice cream. Use vanilla ice cream for the centre. Flavour with 25 g (1 oz) maraschino cherries, halved, and 15 ml (1 tablespoon) syrup from the jar, 15 ml (1-level tablespoon) chopped angelica and 25 g (1 oz) sultanas. Add 5 ml (1 teaspoon) almond essence.

Cherry pom-pom Line the outside with chocolate ice cream. Fill the centre with vanilla ice cream flavoured with 30 ml (2 tablespoons) cherry brandy (or maraschino-flavoured syrup). Dry 8 maraschino-flavoured cherries, dip in melted chocolate, chill, then fold into the ice cream.

Party cooking

Entertaining need hold no terrors when the food has been made ahead of time and stored in the freezer. The hard work and the cost are spread, leaving the hostess time to concentrate on the other part of the job: making sure that the setting is right. Planning is absolutely essential, and it is worth making careful lists to make sure everything is right for the day.

DINNER PARTIES

Plan a menu of tolerant food that will not spoil if left longer than anticipated because your guests are late.

Starters

A cold starter is convenient, and it can be set in place before the guests arrive. Allow for this in the thawing time. Bread rolls can be arranged attractively in a bread basket while still frozen and left to thaw for an hour on the table if the room is warm. Alternatively, warm them in a closed roasting tin in a warm oven for 20 minutes. A slow cooker is ideal for warming bread rolls; they take about $\frac{3}{4}$ hour on the low setting to thaw and warm, but are not harmed by being left longer.

If toast is required for serving with pâté, position the electric toaster on a trolley near the table. Use frozen sliced bread and make as required so that everyone can have hot toast. Make sufficient for half a slice each before the guests sit down and keep it warm in a folded napkin.

Soup is the next most convenient starter to a cold one, because it is easy to heat and serve. Stir in cream, if required, just before serving. Croûtons for serving with the soup can be heated in the oven or under the grill from frozen.

Main courses

Frozen cooked dishes are often covered in sauce to prevent them drying out in the freezer. Compensate by serving a crisp garnish. Take special care in garnishing, using the fresh, crisp foods that do not freeze, such as cucumber, watercress, fresh tomatoes and lettuce.

Avoid serving only frozen vegetables, if possible. If you must, mix them or serve with a sauce to make them different from everyday fare. Sweet corn is useful for adding colour and texture to peas and beans.

Desserts

Thaw desserts in the refrigerator and make sure they are served chilled. Ice cream needs 'tempering' in the frozen food compartment of the refrigerator for several hours before serving. Dish it on to a serving plate and add any necessary decoration while solidly frozen. Make sure the dish will fit into the frozen food compartment.

Cheese

Set the cheeses out attractively on a cheese board. Unwrap all refrigerated and frozen cheeses to let the air mellow them for a few hours. Garnish the cheese with walnuts, grapes and orange wedges complete with skin.

Bake savoury biscuit bites on the day of the dinner party for serving with cheese (see p. 84).

Spring menu (see p. 73)

Salmon seafood pâté
Melba toast

Beef in red wine sauce
Creamed potatoes
Glazed carrots

Frozen oranges
Sugar biscuits

Cheese board
Suggested wine: Burgundy

Preparation

Salmon seafood pâté (see p. 48) Unwrap and leave to thaw overnight in the refrigerator on a serving dish. Garnish the dish with salad vegetables. Garnish the top of the pâté with a row of prawns in shells down the centre and halved slices of cucumber along the sides. Or arrange cucumber cones along the centre. Make these by cutting thin slices of cucumber to their centres, twisting round and pressing to form a cone. Serve chilled with freshly made toast or melba toast.

Melba toast Toast slices of thin sliced bread under a grill until golden brown on both sides. With a sharp knife, cut through the centre to make two very thin slices. Toast the cut sides of each slice (it burns easily, so watch it all the time).

Beef in red wine sauce Thaw red wine cook-in sauce (see p. 40), the day before the dinner party if possible. Add a crushed clove of garlic if desired. Dilute as directed and add to cubes of leg beef in a casserole. Allow 125 g (4 oz) meat for each portion. Cook in a slow oven until the meat is tender — about $1\frac{1}{2}$ hours. Leave to cool, chill in the refrigerator (the flavour will improve if the dish is cooked on the previous day). Serve garnished with chopped parsley and triangles of fried bread or thinly rolled puff pastry cut into crescent shapes and baked.

Serve with fresh or frozen vegetables.

Glazed carrots When the carrots are drained, melt 25 g (1 oz) butter and 10 ml (1 rounded teaspoon) sugar together in a saucepan, increase the heat, add the carrots and shake the pan until the carrots are glazed. Pour into a serving dish and garnish with chopped parsley.

Frozen oranges Follow the recipe on p. 68. Place the oranges in the frozen food compartment of the refrigerator 2 hours before serving. Decorate each with a fresh bay leaf to represent an orange-tree leaf. Serve on a doyley with crisp sugar biscuits.

Summer menu

Cream of cucumber soup

Noisettes of honey roast lamb
Broad beans
Golden new potatoes
Sweet corn

Brandied berry bombe

Suggested wine: Niersteiner

Preparation

Cream of cucumber soup (see p. 46) Serve either hot or cold. Thaw the soup overnight in the refrigerator and whisk while heating, if serving hot, to counteract the slight separation that occurs on freezing. Serve with croûtons. If serving cold, whisk the soup before pouring into bowls. Taste and adjust the seasoning. Float thin slices of cucumber on

▶ A spring dinner party menu: salmon seafood pâté with melba toast, beef in red wine sauce (made from a cook-in sauce) and frozen oranges.

each bowl. Serve with warm rolls and butter.

Noisettes of honey roast lamb (see p. 51) Cut the lamb into six and cook from frozen as directed. Garnish the dish with mint leaves and serve with mint sauce or redcurrant jelly.

Golden new potatoes Rub the skins off some tiny new potatoes. Melt 50 g (2 oz) butter in a large shallow saucepan, add the potatoes, sprinkle with salt, cover with a lid and cook over a low heat, shaking the pan occasionally, until the potatoes are tender and golden brown.

Brandied berry bombe (see p. 68) De-mould on to a serving plate while frozen hard and decorate with piped whipped cream and fruits, if desired. Place in the frozen food compartment of the refrigerator for 2 hours before serving. Serve with crisp sugar biscuits.

Autumn menu

Prawn and melon cocktail

Chicken pie
Runner beans
Anna potatoes

Janne's pavlova

Assorted cheeses
Suggested wine: Piersporter

Preparation

Prawn and melon cocktail Use frozen melon balls and frozen prawns. Thaw slowly, then mix and pile into individual glasses. Garnish each glass with a whole prawn. If the melon is fresh, remove the seeds and cut out the balls with a special scoop, or cut into cubes. Freeze any surplus.

Chicken pie Thaw chicken in ale (see p. 52) and place in a pie dish. Thaw some puff pastry and cover the pie, brush the top with egg and decorate with pastry leaves. Chill until ready to serve then brush with egg again. Place the pie dish on a baking sheet and bake in a hot oven (210°C, 425°F/Gas 7) until the pastry is golden brown.

Anna potatoes Peel 750 g (1½ lb) potatoes in advance and keep in a bowl of cold water. About 1½ hours before serving the meal, melt 100 g (4 oz) butter in a saucepan, brush a shallow ovenproof dish with butter, slice the potatoes very finely and arrange in overlapping layers in a dish. Brush each layer with butter and season well. Cover with buttered grease-proof paper and bake in hot oven (as above) for ¾-1 hour. Serve cut into wedges.

Janne's pavlova (see recipe on p. 60) Unwrap. Thaw on a serving plate. Thaw the fruit for decoration. If using juicy soft fruit such as raspberries, thaw slowly on a plate in the refrigerator and place on the pavlova whilst slightly frozen. Try a peach melba topping: arrange four drained peach halves on top, coat with a little raspberry purée and serve extra in a sauceboat.

Winter menu

Florida cocktail

Chicken in ale
Peas
Duchesse potatoes
Baked parsnips
Strawberry almond cream

Suggested wine:
 Gewurztraminer

Preparation

Florida cocktail Combine an equal quantity of fresh or frozen orange and grapefruit segments. Sprinkle with sugar, if fresh. Serve in halved grapefruit shells and decorate each with a maraschino cherry.

Chicken in ale (see p. 52) Freeze cooked, thaw slowly and cook or heat when required.

Baked parsnips Cut the peeled parsnips in chunks, par-boil, then cook in a little hot fat in a roasting tin on the shelf above the chicken until golden brown.

Duchesse potatoes Cook and sieve the potatoes in advance. Beat in 25 g (1 oz) butter and half a beaten egg to each ½ kg (1 lb) potatoes. Pipe into whirls on a greased baking sheet, brush with the remaining egg and cook in the oven with the chicken until browned. Alternatively, pipe on a baking sheet, open-freeze and store in a freezer bag. To use, brush with egg and cook from frozen.

Strawberry almond cream (see p. 60) Demould and place in the frozen food compartment of the refrigerator for 1 hour before serving. Thaw the strawberry purée and pour into a jug.

BUFFET PARTY FOR FIFTY PEOPLE

Use this party plan for weddings and other large buffet parties. Prepare the food that can be frozen well in advance to leave time for the last-minute finishing. Prepare a batch at a time or you will run short of equipment. Refrigerator space will be limited, so time the removal of some of the food from the freezer very carefully to avoid having to refrigerate too much food. Pâtés, quiches and some gâteaux are often best transported while frozen solid.

When serving a buffet party for as many as fifty people, it is best to put only half the food out at first, removing the plates in due course and re-setting with the remaining food for late-comers. Freeze plenty of sandwiches, vol-au-vents and orange and apple cake (see p. 82) for snacks.

Menu

Boned stuffed turkey
Home-made sausage loaf
Country terrine
Kipper quiche
Washington quiche
Cheese and bacon quiche
Bread rolls
A selection of salads
Chilled citrus cheesecake
Battenberg charlotte
Strawberry cream gâteau
Chocolate profiteroles

Preparation

Boned stuffed turkey (see recipe for boned stuffed chicken on p. 53) Use two 5-kg (11-lb) oven-ready turkeys with suggested turkey stuffing or one 10-kg (24-lb) turkey with double the amount of stuffing. A frozen turkey can be used: it is best to freeze the prepared turkey cooked. To thaw, loosen the wrapping, place on a small board and thaw overnight in a cool larder.

Homemade sausage loaf Adapt the recipe for home-made sausages on pp. 55-6, doubling the quantities. Form the sausagemeat into two large rolls, brush with egg, sprinkle with browned breadcrumbs and bake in a roasting tin in a moderate oven (190°C, 375°F/Gas 5) for $1\frac{1}{4}$-$1\frac{1}{2}$ hours. Cool, chill, freeze and thaw as for boned

stuffed turkey. Serve sliced with chutney.

Savoury quiches (see p. 49) Use foil flan cases. Make double quantities of the basic flavour (four flans) and one quantity of each of the others (four flans). Cut each into eight portions for serving (to allow for second helpings). Leave in the freezer for as long as possible then turn out on to wooden boards; cut into slices while still frozen. Garnish with cress, radishes and cucumber.

Salads Make or buy potato salad and coleslaw. Add some grated carrot to bought coleslaw; garnish the potato salad with snipped chives or parsley. Make four batches of savoury rice (unless you have large, catering-size saucepans). Use 250 g (10 oz) long-grain rice for each batch. Cook the rice, rinse with cold water, then add some strips of canned red pepper, cooked peas, drained pineapple and sliced celery. Moisten with 60 ml (4 tablespoons) bought or homemade French dressing. Arrange tomatoes, cucumber and green salad in other bowls. Serve with mayonnaise and French dressing.

Bread rolls Make or buy these. They are preferable to French bread, which stales quickly. Arrange homemade rolls in bread baskets while still frozen. Cut butter into fancy shapes with a crinkle-cut chip cutter.

Chilled citrus cheesecake (see p. 59) Make two to provide 32 portions. Arrange on serving plates and decor-

▲ Rinsing cooked rice under the tap.

ate while frozen. Try to remove them from the freezer three hours before they are required, to avoid having to refrigerate.

Battenberg charlotte (see p. 60) Make three to provide 24 portions. Arrange on serving plates and decorate with whipped cream while frozen.

Strawberry cream gâteau Adapt the recipe for cream sponge cake on p. 82. Make three to provide 24 portions.

Profiteroles (see p. 65) Prepare 4 times the quantity to provide about 30 portions. Pile into shallow bowls while frozen. Thaw the sauce, pour a little over and serve the remainder in jugs.

Drinks Freeze ice cubes and lemon slices and store in freezer bags for the drinks. Freeze blocks of ice in large plastic containers (2-litre ice-cream containers are useful) for chilling wine. Place the wine in buckets, add the block of ice and fill up with water.

HOT BUFFET FOR TWENTY PEOPLE

Large foil containers of savoury food are quicker, more convenient and more economical to serve than cold food for a party of this number. Soup is a good starter for a winter party, quiche for summer. Serve pâté as an alternative. Make sure that all the food can be eaten with a spoon or a fork —it is very difficult to cut round bones unless sitting at a table.

Menu

Washington quiche
Country terrine

Mild chicken curry
Rice
Lasagne
Green salad

Raspberry almond flan
Black Forest cherry cake

Suggested wine: branded red wine with lasagne, lager with the curry

Preparation

Washington quiche (see p. 50) Make one quantity in two 20-cm (8-in) pie plates. Cut each into 8 to serve.
Country terrine (see p. 48) Thaw overnight in the refrigerator. Serve with bought melba toast.

◀ Hot buffet food for twenty: country terrine or Washington quiche to start, mild chicken curry or lasagne for the main course and Black Forest cherry cake to finish.

Mild chicken curry Make from mild curry cook-in sauce (see p. 42). If serving a greater number, hot curry sauce could be used as well. On the day before the party, cut the meat from two 2-kg (4-lb) chickens, cut into small pieces and cook in the sauce. Use the chicken carcasses to make more stock to freeze. Garnish the dish with gherkins and lemon slices. Serve with boiled rice, using 750 g ($1\frac{1}{2}$ lb) long-grain rice. Cook the rice in two large saucepans on the day before party. Rinse with cold water, drain well, then spread between oiled greaseproof paper and leave in a cool place. Serve the curry with banana slices tossed in lemon juice, sliced tomatoes, natural yoghurt, sliced cucumber and pineapple chunks.
Lasagne (see p. 58) Make one quantity in two party-size square foil dishes. Thaw overnight, then remove the lid and heat when required. Serve with green salad.
Raspberry almond flan (see p. 63) Make in one 30-cm (12-in) or two 20-cm (8-in) flan tins. Thaw during the day of the party. Serve with cream—allow 750 ml ($1\frac{1}{2}$ pints) pouring cream.

Black Forest cherry cake Adapt the recipe for cream sponge cake on p. 82. Double the quantities and replace 25 g (1 oz) flour with 25 g (1 oz) cocoa. Bake in a 22·5-cm (9-in)-deep round cake tin for 35-40 minutes. Divide the cake into three and sprinkle with kirsch. Sandwich two pieces together with a thin layer of whipped cream made from 250 ml ($\frac{1}{2}$ pint) double cream, 125 ml ($\frac{1}{4}$ pint) soured cream and 20 ml (2 rounded teaspoons) castor sugar. Sandwich the other layer with cherry pie filling from a 400-g (14-oz) can (reserve 8 cherries for decoration). Spread a thin layer of cream over the top and side of the cake and open-freeze. Pipe the remaining cream into 16 whirls on foil and freeze; pack the reserved cherries in cling wrap and store separately. Thaw in the refrigerator on the day of the party; sprinkle with grated chocolate, place cream whirls round the edge of the cake; place a cherry on each alternate whirl.

To serve, heat the lasagne in a cool oven (140°C, 275°F/Gas 1) for 2 hours, place the rice in the oven; heat for a further hour.

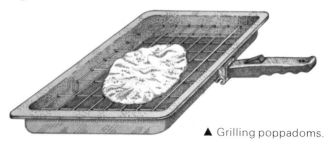

▲ Grilling poppadoms.

Bread, cakes and biscuits

One huge baking day every month is far more practical than short sessions every week. It is as well to include some basic sponge and Victoria sandwich cakes to store ready for decorating. Moist fruit cakes and gingerbreads can be made in roasting tins and stored in bars. Rolls of biscuit dough can be frozen ready for baking and, of course, you need never be without fresh bread if you keep a store in the freezer.

White bread

Bread and the many types of yeasted bun must be served really fresh; a freezer makes this possible. Use fresh or dried yeast. If using fresh yeast mix 25 g (1 oz) with tepid water. For very quick rising, double the yeast quantity and add a crushed 50-mg Vitamin C tablet.

5 ml (1 level teaspoon) castor sugar
100 ml ($\frac{1}{4}$ pint) hand-hot water (43°C, 110°F)
15 ml (1 level tablespoon) dried yeast
25 g (1 oz) lard
1$\frac{1}{2}$ kg (3 lb) plain bread flour
15 ml (1 level tablespoon) salt
60 ml (2 rounded tablespoons) dried milk (optional)

Dissolve the sugar in water in a small basin, add the yeast and leave for about 20 minutes until frothy. Rub the lard into the flour, add the salt and dried milk, if used, then the yeast liquid and 800 ml (1$\frac{1}{4}$ pints) of hand-

hot water all at once. Moisten all the flour by combing through with the hands, then mix to a soft dough. Add more flour if the dough is sticky. Turn out on to a floured board and knead and stretch dough for about 10 minutes until the dough is firm and elastic. Place the dough in covered bowl, in an oiled plastic bag or in a covered saucepan. Leave to rise in a warm place (an airing cupboard) for $\frac{1}{2}$ hour, on the kitchen table for 1 hour or in the refrigerator overnight. Turn out and flatten the dough with the side of the hand, then roll up like a Swiss roll; repeat. Shape the dough in any of the following ways, but keep the dough covered until ready to use.

Tin loaf For small loaf tins (1$\frac{1}{4}$-1$\frac{1}{2}$-pint or 750-800-ml capacity), divide the dough into four. Flatten the dough to a piece the width of the base of the tin. Roll up like a Swiss roll and place in the tin with the join underneath. Brush with oil and place in a plastic bag. Leave until the dough has risen to the top of tin then place on a baking sheet and bake in a very hot oven (230°C, 450°F/Gas 8) for 30-40 minutes until the loaf is brown, has shrunk

from the sides of the tin and sounds hollow when the base is tapped. Cool, pack in freezer bags, excluding air, label, chill and freeze.

To use, thaw at room temperature for about 3 hours or place the loaf in a warm oven for $\frac{1}{2}$ hour. Bread will stale quickly if thawed in the oven.

Bread rolls Use half the dough to make 20 rolls. Shape into plaits, coils, knots or into 12·5-cm (5-in) lengths for finger rolls. Place the baking sheet in a large plastic bag for the dough to rise.

Cottage loaf Use one-quarter of the dough. Cut off one-third of the dough, mould each piece into a ball, place the smaller ball on top of the larger ball and press a floured wooden spoon handle through the centre. Cover, let rise and bake as a tin loaf.

Plait Use one-quarter of the dough. Divide into three and roll each piece between the hands to make 22-cm (9-in) rolls, pointed at the ends and wide at the middle. Place the pieces side by side and start plaiting from the centre, pinch the ends together, turn the dough over and plait the other half. Place on a greased baking sheet. Cover, let rise and bake as a tin loaf.

Croissants Using $\frac{1}{2}$ kg (1 lb) of risen dough, roll out to a strip 45 × 20 cm (18 × 8 in); spread the top two-thirds‚ with 50 g (2 oz) softened butter. Fold the bottom piece, then the top piece, over the centre. Seal the ends, turn the dough so that the fold is on the right side and repeat twice more. Place in a plastic bag and leave in the refrigerator for $\frac{1}{2}$ hour. Divide the dough into two. Roll each piece to a 30-cm (12-in) circle and press a piece of cling wrap over each; leave for 5 minutes, remove the plastic and cut each piece of dough into 6 triangles. Roll each up, long edge towards point, place on a baking sheet and curve into a crescent shape. Place the baking sheet in a

plastic bag and leave the dough to rise in a warm place for about $\frac{1}{2}$ hour, until doubled in size. Brush with beaten egg white and bake in a hot oven (220°C, 425°F/ Gas 7) for 20 minutes.

Pizzas For one large or 4 small basic pizzas, use 450 g (1 lb) risen dough. Press out on an oiled baking sheet into the largest possible circle or divide into four and press out on baking sheets or small sandwich tins. Brush with oil. Cover with a layer of sliced tomato then grated cheese and a sprinkling of mixed dried herbs.

Add any of the following: small sausagemeat balls, cubed luncheon meat, canned mackerel or pilchards, lightly fried onion rings with garlic. Make a lattice of anchovy fillets, strips of bacon or gammon and top with black or green olives. Bake in the centre of a very hot oven (230°C, 450°F/Gas 8) for 20-30 minutes.

To freeze, wrap in foil and store for up to 3 months.

To thaw, heat from frozen in the foil for $\frac{1}{2}$ hour in a moderate oven.

Rich bread dough

Use this recipe for the softest bread rolls and fancy loaves. It also forms the base for many sweet fruited buns and loaves. Use fresh or dried yeast. For quick rising, double the yeast and add a 25-mg Vitamin C tablet for this quantity.

Batter:
    150 g (5 oz) white bread flour

5 ml (1 level teaspoon) sugar
25 g (1 oz) fresh yeast or 10 ml (2 level teaspoons) dried yeast
300 ml (8 fluid oz) warm milk
Dough:
    250 g (11 oz) white bread flour
    5 ml (1 level teaspoon) salt
    50 g (2 oz) margarine
    1 egg

Beat the batter ingredients together; leave in a warm place for 20 minutes until frothy. Place the flour and salt in a bowl and rub in the margarine. Add to the batter with the egg and mix to a soft dough. Turn on to the table and knead for 5 minutes until the dough is firm and no longer sticky. Use for loaves, rolls (see white bread recipe, p. 78), freezer rolls, doughnuts or hot cross buns.

Freezer rolls These part-baked rolls can be made from plain white or rich bread dough. Make as in the previous recipes but bake in a cool oven (120°C, 225°F/ Gas $\frac{1}{2}$) for $\frac{1}{2}$ hour to set dough. Cool and pack in freezer bags. Store for up to 3 months.

To use, bake from frozen in a pre-heated hot oven (200°C, 400°F/Gas 6) until browned — about 15 minutes.

Doughnuts For round doughnuts, grease 16 bun tins. For long ones, use a baking sheet. Form rich bread dough into 16 balls or 10-cm (4-in) rolls, place in bun tins or on a baking sheet and leave to rise in greased plastic bags. Heat a deep-fat pan to 182°C, 360°F, and mix 5 ml (1 level teaspoon) cinnamon and 60 ml (2 rounded tablespoons) castor sugar on a plate. Fry the doughnuts four at a time, drain on kitchen paper then quickly roll in the sugar mixture; cool.

To serve, split and fill with jam and/or whipped cream.

To freeze, open-freeze then wrap individually in cling wrap and pack in freezer bags. Store for up to 3 months.

To thaw, unwrap and thaw at room temperature for 3-4 hours.

Hot cross buns Press out the rich bread dough to a large square, sprinkle with a mixture of 150 g (6 oz) currants, 50 g (2 oz) sultanas, 5 ml (1 level teaspoon) mixed spice and 50 g (2 oz) icing sugar. Roll up like a Swiss roll then press out and roll up again. Divide into 16 pieces, roll each into a ball, place on greased baking sheets and brush with a glaze made by dissolving 30 ml (1 rounded tablespoon) sugar in 90 ml (6 tablespoons) milk. Score a cross on the top of each with a sharp knife. Cover

and leave to rise until doubled in size. Bake in a hot oven (200°C, 400°F/Gas 6) for about $\frac{1}{2}$ hour.

To freeze, cool, chill, pack into freezer bags, store for up to 3 months.

To use, heat from frozen in a covered roasting tin for $\frac{1}{2}$ hour in a moderate oven. Glaze before serving.

Note Fruit and spice mix may be added with dough ingredients.

Prune and orange tea loaf
Makes 2 loaves
150 g (6 oz) sugar
250 ml ($\frac{1}{2}$ pint) milk
150 g (6 oz) pitted prunes
200 g (8 oz) thick-cut
  marmalade
300 g (12 oz) self-raising
  flour
5 ml (1 level teaspoon)
  ground coriander or
  allspice
Grease and line the base of two 1-lb (1$\frac{1}{2}$-pint or 1-litre capacity) loaf tins. Prepare a moderate oven (180°C, 350°F/Gas 4). Dissolve the sugar in the milk in a saucepan, remove from the heat, add the halved prunes and marmalade and leave to cool. Sift the flour and spice together and add to the pan, divide between the tins and bake in the centre of the oven for $\frac{3}{4}$-1 hour. Serve sliced and buttered.

To freeze Wrap in foil, label, chill and store for up to 6 months.

Moist chocolate cake
This cake improves with keeping. For a sweeter cake, fill with apricot jam or butter

icing and top with glacé icing or chocolate.
50 g (2 oz) cocoa
150 g (6 oz) self-raising
  flour
5 ml (1 level teaspoon)
  baking powder .
5 ml (1 level teaspoon)
  cinnamon
100 g (4 oz) castor sugar
45 ml (3 level tablespoons)
  golden syrup
15 ml (1 level tablespoon)
  black treacle
4 eggs
200 g (8 oz) soft margarine
Prepare a moderate oven (160°C, 325°F/Gas 3). Grease and line the base of a 17·5-cm (7-in) round cake tin. Sift the cocoa, flour, baking powder and cinnamon into a bowl. Add the remaining ingredients. Be sure to measure the syrup and treacle very carefully. Mix together, then beat for 1-2 minutes until the mixture is glossy. Spread in the tin and bake in the centre of the oven for $1\frac{1}{4}$-$1\frac{1}{2}$ hours. Leave to cool in the tin for $\frac{1}{2}$ hour, then turn out, remove the paper and leave to cool completely. Split and ice, if desired, then pack in a rigid box. (Place on the lid and open-freeze if the decoration might otherwise be damaged.) Wrap in foil if not iced. Store for 3 months.

► In the foreground, pizzas; behind them, sweet and savoury biscuit rolls for slicing from frozen; cooling on the rack, nutty biscuit roll, savoury biscuit bites and gingernut biscuit roll; in the centre, orange and apple cake, lemon cream sponge.

Orange and apple cake
(see p. 81)

1 large thin-skinned orange of about 200 g ($\frac{1}{2}$ lb)
250 ml ($\frac{1}{2}$ pint) tea or dry white wine
400 g (1 lb) mixed dried fruit
300 g (12 oz) prepared cooking apples
400 g (1 lb) castor sugar
300 g (12 oz) margarine
4 eggs
500 g (1$\frac{1}{4}$ lb) plain flour
15 ml (1 level tablespoon) baking powder
10 ml (2 level teaspoons) cinnamon

Scrub the orange, cut into pieces, remove the pips, then chop finely or liquidize with the tea or wine until the orange is finely chopped. Then add any pieces of dried fruit that require chopping. Pour the orange, tea or wine into a saucepan, bring to the boil, cover and simmer for 10 minutes. Remove from the heat, add the dried fruit, then leave to cool, stirring occasionally. Cut the prepared apple into small cubes and add to the saucepan. Prepare a moderate oven (180°C, 350°F/Gas 4). Line a large (2$\frac{1}{2}$-litre or 5$\frac{1}{2}$-pint) roasting tin with greaseproof paper; grease the tin and paper. Cream the sugar and margarine together until light and fluffy. Beat in the eggs one at a time. Sift the flour, baking powder and cinnamon together and mix, alternating with the fruit mixture, into the creamed mixture. Spread in the tin and level the surface. Bake in the centre of the oven for 1$\frac{1}{2}$-1$\frac{3}{4}$ hours. Test by pressing with the fingers. The cake should spring back and have begun to shrink from the tin. Leave to cool in the tin, then turn out and remove the paper.

To freeze Cut into slices or squares; interleave with greaseproof paper or plastic tissue. Wrap in small foil parcels. Label, chill and freeze. The cake will store for up to 4 months.

To use Remove the number of slices required, thaw at room temperature or wrap in foil and heat in a steamer for 20 minutes.

Wholewheat ginger cake
250 ml ($\frac{1}{2}$ pint) milk
200 g (8 oz) granulated sugar
200 g (8 oz) golden syrup
200 g (8 oz) black treacle
200 ml (8 fluid oz) oil
200 g (8 oz) plain white flour
5 ml (1 level teaspoon) bicarbonate of soda
30 ml (2 level tablespoons) ground ginger
15 ml (1 level tablespoon) mixed spice
200 g (8 oz) plain wholewheat flour
200 g (8 oz) seedless raisins

Grease a large 30 × 25 cm (12 × 10 in) roasting tin; line the base with greaseproof paper. Prepare a cool oven (150°C, 300°F/Gas 2). Place the milk and sugar in a large saucepan; stir over a low heat until the sugar has melted. Remove from the heat and add the syrup, treacle and oil; sitr well until mixed. Sift the flour, bicarbonate of soda, ginger and mixed spice together and add to the saucepan with the wholewheat flour; mix until smooth, then stir in the raisins and pour into the prepared tin. Bake just above the centre of the oven for 1$\frac{3}{4}$-2 hours. Leave to cool in the tin for $\frac{1}{2}$ hour then turn out, remove the paper and leave to cool completely.

To freeze Cut into bars and pack in cling wrap. Pack in to freezer bags. Store for up to 3 months.

To use Remove each bar as required. Leave to thaw for 1 hour at room temperature, then cut into squares and leave to thaw completely.

Cream sponge cake
Fresh cream cakes are well worth storing in the freezer. This basic recipe can be flavoured and shaped in many ways.

Sponge:
2 eggs
50 g (2 oz) castor sugar
50 g (2 oz) plain flour
2·5 ml ($\frac{1}{2}$ level teaspoon) baking powder

Filling:
125 ml ($\frac{1}{4}$ pint) double cream
5 ml (1 level teaspoon) sugar
jam

Prepare a moderate oven (190°C, 375°F/Gas 5). Grease and line one 20-cm (8-in) tin or two 17·5-cm (7-in) tins. Whisk the eggs and sugar until thick (do this over a bowl of hot water if using a hand whisk). Sift the flour and baking powder over the surface then gently cut through the mixture with a large metal spoon until combined. Pour into the

tin(s), shake to level the surface, then bake in the centre of the oven until risen and golden – 15-30 minutes. Turn out, remove the paper and cool. Whisk the cream and sugar together until stiff and sandwich the cake with jam and cream.
To freeze Wrap in foil, label and chill. Store for up to 4 months.
To use Thaw, then dredge with icing sugar.

Variations
Fruit cream cake Spread cream and a layer of raspberries, peaches (blanched) or canned fruit on the cake. Pack some fruit separately for decoration.
Fruit gâteau In addition to putting cream and jam in the centre, decorate the top with piped cream, using an extra 125 ml ($\frac{1}{4}$ pint) cream and fruit. Open-freeze, then pack in a rigid box. Or freeze undecorated and freeze the cream in whirls (see p. 27). Place on the gâteau to thaw.
Lemon cream sponge (see p. 81) Make the cake as above but spread the base and top with lemon curd. Pipe a lattice of cream on top and open-freeze. Pack in a rigid box. Decorate with fresh lemon slices just before serving.
Honey fudge cake Bake the cake in two 17·5-cm (7-in) tins; cut each into two. Fill the cakes, then sandwich together (making three layers) with lemon butter icing using 100 g (4 oz) butter, 200 g (8 oz) icing sugar, lemon rind and 30 ml (2 tablespoons) juice. Make

fudge frosting by melting 100 g (4 oz) butter in a saucepan with 30 ml (2 tablespoons) milk and 15 ml (1 tablespoon) clear honey. Bring to the boil, remove from the heat and stir in 300 g (12 oz) sifted icing sugar. Beat until the mixture cools and thickens, then pour over the cake and leave to set. Decorate with browned flaked almonds.
To freeze, open-freeze then pack in a rigid box.
To thaw, place on a plate and thaw at room temperature (the icing will go very wet, but will dry as it thaws).
Apricot cream bar Bake the cake in a 17·5×25-cm (7×10-in) Swiss roll tin for about 10 minutes. Invert on sugared greaseproof paper, remove the paper and leave to cool. Cut in half lengthwise. Sandwich the cake with sieved, warm apricot jam and half the cream. Spread the top layer and sides with apricot jam then press chopped, toasted hazelnuts on to the sides. Arrange rows of halved, canned apricots over the top and decorate the edges with piped, whipped cream.
Swiss roll Bake as above, trim the edges with a sharp knife, spread with jam and roll up. Or roll up with

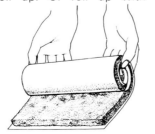

greaseproof paper inside, unroll when cool and fill with butter icing or fruit and cream. Decorate the top with alternate rows of fruit and cream or flavoured butter icing.
To make a chocolate-flavoured Swiss roll, replace 15 ml (1 level tablespoon) flour with cocoa.

Foolproof baked custard tart
A frozen custard bakes perfectly – the pastry is cooked while the custard thaws and slowly cooks. Use whole eggs or just the yolks, saving the whites for a pavlova.
Makes 2
shortcrust pastry using 300 g (12 oz) flour
6 eggs or egg yolks
5 ml (1 teaspoon) vanilla essence
75 g (3 oz) sugar
750 ml (1$\frac{1}{2}$ pints) milk
grated nutmeg
Line two foil 21·8-cm (8$\frac{3}{4}$-in) round pie plates with pastry, allowing the pastry to overlap the rim by 1·25 cm ($\frac{1}{2}$ in). Turn under the pastry at the edge of each and pull up with the fingers to form a ridge higher than the edge of the plate; flute with the fingers. Chill while making the filling. Beat the eggs or egg yolks, vanilla and sugar together. Gradually beat in the milk. Place the foil plates on baking sheets, divide the custard between them (it's easier to do this in the freezer) and grate some nutmeg on top. Open-freeze until firm then over-wrap the plates and store for up to 3 months.

To bake Unwrap, place the plates of frozen tarts on baking sheets in the oven, set the oven to moderate (190°C, 375°F/Gas 5) and bake for about 1 hour until the pastry is golden brown and the custard is just firm. Take care not to overcook. If the oven has been pre-heated, cook for 10 minutes less.

Note Alternatively, line individual round pie dishes 8 cm (3½ in) across, 3 cm (1¼ in) deep. Bake for 30-40 minutes.

Savoury biscuit bites

(see p. 81)
Makes about 120

200 g (8 oz) plain flour
100 g (4 oz) ground rice
15 ml (1 level tablespoon) dry mustard
10 ml (1 rounded teaspoon salt
pinch cayenne pepper
150 g (6 oz) margarine
150 g (6 oz) Cheddar cheese
1 egg
5 ml (1 level teaspoon) paprika
5 ml (1 level teaspoon) poppy seeds
vegetable extract

Mix the flour, ground rice, mustard, salt and pepper. Rub in the margarine, then add the cheese and beaten egg and mix to a stiff dough. Divide into four. Knead the paprika into half of one piece, form into a roll 18 cm (7½ in) long. Roll out the remaining half of the piece to an oblong the same length and 7·5 cm (3 in) wide. Place the paprika-flavoured piece on top and roll up together; press the

join together to seal. Repeat with another piece and the poppy seeds. Roll out the third piece to an oblong 18 × 12·5 cm (7 × 5 in). Spread with the vegetable extract then roll up like a Swiss roll. Form the remaining piece into a roll 18 cm (7½ in) long.

To use Chill, slice and bake in a moderate oven (180°C, 350°F/Gas 4) until golden brown – about 15 minutes.

To freeze Pack each roll in cling wrap. Store in a freezer bag for up to 3 months.

Note Make plain biscuits larger for serving with cheese.

Gingernut biscuit roll

(see p. 81)

100 g (4 oz) golden syrup
100 g (4 oz) black treacle
150 g (6 oz) margarine
400 g (1 lb) self-raising flour
30 ml (2 level tablespoons) ground ginger
15 ml (1 level tablespoon) mixed spice
10 ml (2 level teaspoons) bicarbonate of soda
200 g (8 oz) castor sugar
2 eggs

Warm the syrup, treacle and margarine together until melted; cool. Sift the flour, ginger, spice and bicarbonate of soda into a bowl. Add the sugar and eggs. Add the cooled syrup mixture and mix well. Place the bowl in the refrigerator and leave until thoroughly chilled. Divide into four pieces on a floured board and roll each between the hands to a sausage shape, about 5 cm (2 in) in diameter.

To use Cut into slices about 1 cm (½ in) thick, improve the shape with the fingers and place on a greased baking sheet, allowing room for spreading. Bake in a moderate oven (160°C, 325°F/Gas 3) for 15-20 minutes. Cool for 2 minutes. Place on a wire rack.

To freeze Pack each roll in cling wrap, then pack in a freezer bag. Store for up to 3 months. Slice and bake when frozen.

Nutty biscuit roll

(see p. 81)
Store this roll in the freezer then cut and bake slices as required.

300 g (12 oz) plain flour
100 g (4 oz) ground rice
90 ml (6 level tablespoons) crunchy peanut butter
200 g (8 oz) soft margarine
250 g (10 oz) castor sugar
10 ml (2 level teaspoons) baking powder
30 ml (2 tablespoons) milk
25 g (1 oz) plain chocolate (optional)

Mix all the ingredients except the chocolate. Chop the chocolate, if used, and add to half of the mixture. Form the mixture into two rolls, each about 5 cm (2 in) in diameter. Pack in cling wrap and chill.

To use Cut thin slices and bake on greased baking sheets in a moderate oven (180°C, 350°F/Gas 4) for 15-20 minutes until pale golden brown.

To freeze Pack the rolls in freezer bags. Thaw slightly and slice when required, returning the remainder to the freezer.

Storage times

These maximum recommended storage times indicate how long frozen food will keep without flavour and texture deterioration. There will be no harmful effects if food is stored for longer, but it will not taste so good. Fluctuating temperatures in the freezer and poor packaging reduce the storage times.

MEAT

Beef	12 months
Lamb	10 months
Veal	9 months
Pork	9 months
Bacon joints:	
unsmoked	5 weeks
smoked	8 weeks
Bacon rashers:	
unsmoked	2 weeks
smoked	4 weeks
Mince	2-3 months
Offal and tripe	2 months
Sausages	6 weeks

Note Bacon will store for longer if vacuum packed.

POULTRY AND GAME

Chicken	12 months
Turkey	9 months
Duck	9 months
Goose	9 months
Venison	6-8 months
Game	6-8 months
Giblets	3 months

FISH

White fish	12 months
Oily fish (herrings, mackerel trout, salmon)	9 months
Shellfish	1 month

DAIRY PRODUCE

Butter:	
unsalted	6 months
salted	4 months
Lard	6 months
Margarine	12 months
Eggs:	
whole or yolks	6 months
whites	12 months
Cream (whipped, double or clotted)	4 months
Cream whirls	2 months
Milk:	
homogenized	6 months
pasteurized	3 months
raw	2 months
Cheese:	
hard	6 months
grated	4 months
soft and cottage	4 months
Ice cream	3 months

BAKED FOODS

Bread	6 months
Rich breads and buns	4 months
Pastry:	
cooked	6 months
raw	3-4 months
Cakes:	
fatless	12 months
made with fat	6 months
fruit	6-12 months
gingerbread	4 months
Biscuits	4 months

PREPARED DISHES

(soups, stews, pâtés, etc.)	3 months

FRUIT

Most fruits	12 months
Fruit purée	10 months
Rhubarb	10 months

VEGETABLES

Blanched	12 months
Fried (chipped potatoes, mushrooms and courgettes)	6 months

TO GAIN MAXIMUM STORAGE TIME

Good freezer management can extend the storage times listed. Remember the following points:

1. Choose only good-quality food for freezing. Poor-quality food is not improved by freezing, nor is it worth the cost of storage or packaging.

2. Food must be fresh or freshly cooked. To avoid contaminating the food, take particular care with kitchen hygiene when preparing foods for freezing. Cool stews, soups and casseroles quickly in iced water. Micro-organisms multiply rapidly in warm temperatures.

3. Pack food in vapour- and moisture-proof material to prevent it drying out.

4. Remove air from the package to avoid oxidation of the food.

5. Aim to freeze food as quickly as possible, remembering the following points:

(a) pack food in thin packages;

(b) operate the fast-freeze switch 1 hour before freezing any fresh food unless only 1 kg (2 lb) of food is being frozen;

(c) isolate the food from any surrounding frozen food and position each package next to the freezing surface;

(d) do not overload the freezer.

Fruits and vegetables for freezing

FRUITS

Apples Bramley Seedling.
Blackcurrants Boskoop Giant, Laxton Giant, Blacksmith, Wellington, Tenah, Malling Jet.
Gooseberries Careless, Whinhams Industry.
Greengages Cambridge Gage, Jefferson, Comte d' Althan's Gage.
Peaches Hale's Early.
Plums Victoria and purple varieties.
Raspberries Norfolk Giant, Lloyd George, Malling Enterprise, Malling Jewel, Malling Promise.
Redcurrants Jonkheer Van Tets.
Strawberries Cambridge Favourite, Cambridge Vigour, Cambridge Prizewinner, Redgauntlet, Royal Sovereign, Carnival, French Alpine.
Tomatoes Gardener's Delight.

VEGETABLES

Asparagus Connover's Colossal.
Beans, broad The Sutton, Imperial Green Windsor, Imperial White Windsor.
Beans, French The Prince, Tendergreen, Masterpiece, Cordon.
Beans, runner Achievement, Prizewinner, Kelvedon Wonder, Kelvedon Marvel, Streamline, Fry, Hammond's Dwarf White.
Brussels sprouts Peer Gynt, Prince Askold, Roodnerf Stiekema Early, Roodnerf Seven Hills.

Calabrese (broccoli) Express Corona F1, Green Comet F1, Italian Sprouting.
Carrots Amsterdam Forcing.
Cauliflower All the Year Round, Snowball, South Pacific, English Winter St George.
Peas Little Marvel, Early Onward, Kelvedon Wonder, Onward.
Seakale beet Silver Beet.
Spinach Long-standing round, New Zealand Spinach.
Sweet corn John Innes F1, Earliking F1, Kelvedon Glory F1, North Star F1, Early Extra Sweet F1.

PREPARATION OF FRUIT FOR FREEZING

Apples

1. In slices Slice peeled, cored apples into boiling water or sugar syrup. Leave until pliable (about 1 minute) then remove with a draining spoon, dry on kitchen paper and pack in bags or boxes. Chill, label and freeze.

Use blanched slices to make pies. Layer slices with sugar and freeze pies uncooked.

2. As purée Wash apples and chop. Cook, without peeling, in the minimum amount of water. Press through a nylon sieve. Sweeten to taste. Freeze in containers. Remove frozen block if containers are limited. For apple sauce, freeze purée in small containers or in ice-cube trays. Remove cubes and pack in freezer bags for storage.

3. Whole Freeze apples for homemade wine this way. They break down when thawed, which assists the flavour extraction. Wash apples, dry, then pack in freezer bags.

Apricots

Cut in halves, remove stones and pack in sugar or syrup.
To use Poach in own syrup or thaw and use in pies.

Bananas

Do not freeze whole. Mash, mix with sugar and lemon juice. Use 30 ml (1 rounded tablespoon) sugar and 5 ml (1 teaspoon) lemon juice to each banana. Pack in small containers.
To use Thaw in covered container in refrigerator overnight. Use in trifles, cakes, tea loaves, cake fillings.

Blackberries

1. Open-freeze For cultivated blackberries. Pack in bags or boxes, thaw in refrigerator and use raw.
2. In dry sugar For pies and stewed fruit. Mix with blanched apples, if desired. Thaw before making pies. If making pies for freezing, layer pie with sugar.
3. For jam Pack dry in weighed amounts. Add a little extra fruit.

Blackcurrants

Blanch in boiling water for ½ minute to prevent skins toughening. Freeze as for blackberries. May also be frozen in syrup.

Blueberries, bilberries or whortleberries
As for blackcurrants. Add some lemon juice to the syrup.

Cherries
Remove stones if storing for longer than 4 months. Pack in syrup. Cook acid varieties from frozen, thaw dessert varieties in unopened container.

Citrus fruits (oranges, grapefruit, lemons, tangerines, etc.)
1. In segments Cut off rind, then cut between segments with a sharp knife to avoid any pith. Layer in containers with sugar. Use for fruit cocktails or salads.
2. Juice Pack in usable amounts in cartons.
3. Slices Lemon and orange slices are especially useful for drinks or garnish. Separate with plastic tissue and use frozen.
4. Whole For marmalade. Wrap individually in cling wrap and pack in a freezer bag. Pack extra fruit to compensate for loss of pectin during storage. Cook while frozen to retain colour.
5. Peel Grate the peel and store in twists of cling wrap in a freezer bag. Add frozen to cakes and desserts for flavour.

Gooseberries
1. Whole Pack into freezer bags. Top and tail either before

or after freezing. Stew from frozen or thaw and use in pies.
2. Stewed If space is limited, stew the fruit before freezing in containers.

Melon
Peel and remove seeds. Cut into cubes or balls using a baller gadget. Freeze in syrup with lemon juice or ginger added for flavour. Thaw slowly in container and use while chilled.

Peaches
Blanch for $\frac{1}{2}$ minute in boiling water, cool immediately, then peel. Drop halves or slices immediately into sugar syrup with ascorbic acid added.

Plums
1. Whole Pack in freezer bags. Remove stones if they are to be frozen for more than 6 months. Stew from frozen to retain colour.

2. Halved This is best for stoned, light-coloured plums. Add ascorbic acid to the syrup.

Redcurrants
Purée Cook and rub through a sieve. Pack into tubs.
Whole For decoration. Leave the stalks on.
For jelly Pack with the stalks on: they are easier to remove when frozen. Pack in freezer bags with extra fruit to allow for loss of pectin during storage.

Rhubarb
Stewed Pack into cartons.
Chunks Blanch for 1 minute, then pack in syrup.

Soft fruits
Whole This is the best way of freezing raspberries and loganberries. Open-freeze, then pack into containers; roll in castor sugar first, if desired.
Sliced This is good for strawberries. Layer with sugar to keep firm.
Purée This is an ideal way to freeze strawberries. Pack in tubs.

Freezing calendar

January
Citrus fruits are at their best. Freeze orange and grapefruit segments and juice, lemon slices, Seville oranges.

February
Fresh vegetables are not very plentiful, so use some of your stock of frozen vegetables. Mix them for a change. Make and freeze pies with early pink rhubarb. Oranges can be added to rhubarb desserts. Make pancakes in advance for Shrove Tuesday.

March
Freeze purple sprouting broccoli if there is a surplus.
Stock up the freezer with baked foods. Make desserts and gâteaux for Easter entertaining. Make hot cross buns for serving on Good Friday.

April
Make lemon and orange curd and store in small containers.
Make biscuit rolls for entertaining.
Check the dates on packages of food and use up the older packs in preparation for cleaning and defrosting the freezer.

May
Defrost the freezer this month in preparation for the forthcoming harvest. Re-write your stock records.
Make a selection of snack meals suitable for picnics.
Freeze surplus rhubarb.

June
Freeze new potatoes, peas, herbs, gooseberries and strawberries.
Make fruit water ices.
Make freezer preserve with strawberries.

July
Freeze raspberries, currants, plums, carrots, peas, broad beans, French beans, herbs, courgettes. Use surplus cucumbers to make purée for soup.

August
Make purées from mature soft fruits and tomatoes. Mix windfall apples with soft fruits in pies. Pick and freeze blackberries. Freeze plums, sweet corn, runner beans and courgettes. Make ratatouille with mixed vegetables. Buy the turkey for Christmas.

September
Freeze surplus apples; make some into pie fillings.
Freeze damson, tomatoes, peppers. Freeze fruits, especially elderberries for wine-making.

October
Freeze mixed root vegetables ready prepared for soups.
Stock up on meat and basic foods.
Make dishes for entertaining.

November
Make cook-in sauces to help with quick meals for the busy period of Christmas preparation.
Make lists for Christmas cooking and start the preparations.

December
Make and freeze mince pies; make stuffings, breadcrumbs, cakes, gâteaux and puddings for Christmas. Freeze a spectacular dessert for Christmas Day as an alternative to the traditional pudding. Make trifles.
Make pâté and pack it in attractive dishes for presents. Label with thawing instructions.

Metrication

Solid measure
Both metric and imperial quantities are given in the recipes and methods in this book. Use either metric or imperial: do *not* mix them.
For large amounts, the equivalents are as follows:

1 kg (1,000 g)	= 2 lb
$\frac{1}{2}$ kg (500 g)	= 1 lb
$\frac{1}{4}$ kg (250 g)	= $\frac{1}{2}$ lb (8 oz)
125 g	= 4 oz
50 g	= 2 oz
25 g	= 1 oz

For small amounts up to 1 lb:

400 g	= 1 lb
200 g	= $\frac{1}{2}$ lb (8 oz)
100 g	= 4 oz
50 g	= 2 oz
25 g	= 1 oz

Liquid measure
One pint equals 0·568 litres. The metric amount has been rounded down to 0·500 litres or 500 millilitres (abbreviated to ml):

1 litre (1,000 ml)	= 2 pints
$\frac{1}{2}$ litre (500 ml)	= 1 pint
250 ml	= $\frac{1}{2}$ pint
125 ml	= $\frac{1}{4}$ pint

Spoon measure
Metric measuring spoons have been used for the recipes in this book. These give a very accurate measurement, which is especially important when measuring strong ingredients such as spices. The spoons are calibrated by volume.

15-ml spoon	= 1 level tablespoon
10-ml spoon	= 1 level dessertspoon
5-ml spoon	= 1 level teaspoon
2·5-ml spoon	= $\frac{1}{2}$ level teaspoon

Vegetable blanching chart

Vegetable	Preparation	Blanching and cooling time		Freezing method
asparagus	Grade for size	thin	2 minutes	Pack into containers
		thick	4 minutes	
beans:				
broad	Shell, and grade for size	small	2 minutes	Pack in freezer bags
		large	3 minutes	
French	Trim ends; cut in chunks if desired	whole	3 minutes	Open-freeze; pack in bags
		cut	2 minutes	
runner	String, if necessary; cut into chunks	2 minutes		As French beans
broccoli	Grade for size; soak 30 minutes in cold salt water	3 to 4 minutes		Open-freeze; pack in boxes
Brussels sprouts	Grade for size: small sprouts are best. Soak 30 minutes in cold salt water	3 minutes		Open-freeze; pack in bags or boxes
carrots	Freeze only small, young carrots; scrub and trim	5 minutes		Rub off skins; pack in bags
cauliflower	Break into florets	3 minutes		Open-freeze; pack in bags
courgettes	Cut into 2-cm (1-in) lengths	3 minutes		Open-freeze; pack in bags
mushrooms	Wash and dry; cut in quarters if large	(a) Fry in butter (b) Do not blanch		(a) Pack in containers (b) Open-freeze
peas	Shell and grade into sizes	1 minute		Open-freeze
peppers	Wash; cut in halves; remove seeds and membrane; slice	2 minutes		Pack into bags or boxes
potatoes:				
new	Choose small potatoes	Until almost cooked		Pack in bags
chipped	Fry until almost cooked but not browned	Cool quickly		Open-freeze; pack in bags
spinach	Prepare as for serving	2 minutes; stir		Pack in bags
mixed vegetables	Prepare each vegetable separately; then mix	Blanch separately		Pack in bags

Suppliers

PACKAGING

Most stationers, freezer centres, some supermarkets and some stationery departments of large stores sell packaging for home freezing. Others supply equipment by mail order and issue catalogues. In the list below, the brand names appear first, in italics.

Alcan
Alcan Polyfoil Ltd,
P.O. Box 3,
Chesham,
Buckinghamshire
02405 6061

Bettapak
Hereford 0432 67631

Coldstore
Packaging Ltd,
21 Foregate,
Kilmarnock
KA1 1LU

Frigicold
Lonsdale Uniflair Ltd,
4-6 Sergeants Way,
Caxton Road,
Bedford
MK41 0EH
0234 41366

Garfrost
William Garfield Ltd,
Florence Street,
Birmingham
B1 1NX
021 622 2303

Lakeland
Lakeland Plastics,
99 Alexandra Road,
Windermere
Windermere 2255
Mail order only: well-designed colour-coded equipment as well as general packaging.

Lamifoil
Ready Freeze Ltd,
Belvedere Road,
Lowestoft,
Suffolk
0502 61731

Stayfrost
Stayfrost Ltd,
58 Blatchington Road,
Hove,
BN3 3YH
0273 721144

Stewart
Stewart Plastics Ltd,
Purley Way,
Croydon,
Surrey

Swantex
Icefresh
Swan Mill Paper Co. Ltd,
Swan Mills,
Swanley,
Kent
0322 65566

Thorpac
Thorpac Ltd,
Cirencester,
Gloucestershire
0285 4249

Tupperware
Tupperware Ltd,
P.O. Box 80,
High Wycombe,
Buckinghamshire
HP11 2TA
Well-designed, good-quality plastic containers with airtight seals.

BAG SEALERS

Easiseal
D.R.G. Packaging Ltd,
Elsynge House,
Forty Hill,
Enfield,
Middlesex

Siemens
Siemens Ltd,
Domestic Appliance Division,
Great West House,
Great West Road,
Brentford,
Middlesex
01-568 9133

FREEZER BASKETS

Floral
Floral Foundations Ltd,
Caldervale Works,
River Street,
Brighouse,
Yorkshire
HD6 1JS
Brighouse 2641

Hamster
Hamster Baskets,
Dept. FF3,
Much Marcle,
Ledbury,
Herefordshire
Trumpet 209
This company will make any size or shape of basket to order. Before ordering, take particular care to read the company's instructions on how to measure the freezer.

FREEZER THERMOMETERS

See Frigicold, Lakeland Plastics and Stayfrost, all listed under packaging.

MEAT THERMOMETERS

Swedish Marketing Ltd,
Rumbow House,
Halesowen,
Worcestershire

ICE CREAM-MAKING EQUIPMENT

Divertimenti,
68 & 70 Marylebone Lane,
London
W1M 5FF
01-935 0689
This company stocks an electrically-operated bucket churn for large quantities of ice cream, also a shallow ice-cream maker that fits into the frozen food compartment of the refrigerator. Divertimenti also stocks ice-cream brick moulds and copper bombe moulds.

Book list and films

There is a wealth of material on freezing, in freezer centres, bookshops and libraries. Besides the many books and brochures, several magazines run features on the subject, there are two magazines which specialize in information and recipes on freezing, and some of the freezer centres publish monthly newspapers with news of special offers and ideas for seasonal catering.

The Encyclopaedia of Home Freezing, Audrey Ellis, Hamlyn, 1977, £4·95.
This author has written books on every aspect of freezing and this helpful volume comprises all the essential information on the subject.

Good Housekeeping Home Freezer Cook Book, The Good Housekeeping Institute, Ebury Press, 1972, £3·25.
A comprehensive book covering every aspect of home freezing, including recipes.

The Freezer Book, Marye Cameron-Smith, Elm Tree Books, 1973, £2·75.
This book is an invaluable guide to buying and using a freezer. Correct freezing technique is explained in detail. There are many interesting recipes, from hors d'oeuvres to desserts, and a large section of cakes and bakes.

Freezer Facts, Margaret Leach, Forbes Publications, 1975, £4·85.
No school library should be without this book. The result of many years of research pioneered by the author and her colleagues at the Home Food Storage and Preservation section of the University of Bristol at Long Ashton Research Station, it explains in great detail what happens to food when it is frozen.

The Home Book of Food Freezing, Pat M. Cox, Faber Paperbacks, 1977, £2·50.
Detailed information on freezers and freezing with a recipe section which includes many classic dishes.

A Guide to Home Freezing, Jeni Wright, Octopus, 1977, £3·95.
The beautiful illustrations, of both freezing methods and recipes, make this book a good buy for both new and established freezer owners.

ABC of Home Freezing (MAFS Bulletin no. 214) Her Majesty's Stationery Office, 1978, £1·75.
This technical paperback includes all the latest research on home freezing carried out by the Home Food Storage and Preservation Section at Long Ashton Research Station, University of Bristol.

Food Freezing at Home, Gwen Conacher, The Electricity Council, 35p.
Good, sound information. This inexpensive handbook on freezing and freezers has outsold all other freezer books and has even been translated into Braille.

You and Your Freezer, Jess Mitchell, Hutchinson Benham, 1977, 60p.
An interesting book with especially good information on buying and freezing meat.

Growing, Freezing and Cooking, Keith Mossman and Mary Norwak, Elm Tree Books, 1974, £2·50 (hardback) and Sphere Books, 1974, 85p.
Contains an alphabetical guide to many vegetables, herbs and fruits with advice on cultivation, varieties and freezing.

Complete Book of Freezer Cooking, Mary Berry, Octopus, 1975, £2·50.
Explains how to use a freezer and contains many colour illustrations and recipes with full instructions for preparing, freezing, thawing and serving.

MAGAZINES
Home & Freezer Digest (monthly), published by British European Associated Publications Ltd.

The Freezer Family (bi-monthly), published by Retail Journals Ltd.

Freeze (quarterly), published by Hereford Press Ltd.

LEAFLETS
British Meat and the Home Freezer, 30p, from The Meat and Livestock Commission, 5 St John's Square, London EC1.

The New Zealand Lamb Guide to Home Freezing, free from The New Zealand Lamb Bureau, 80-82 Cromer Street, London WC1.

Home Freezing of Bread and Flour Products, free from the Flour Advisory Bureau, 21 Arlington Street, London SW1.

The Food Freezer and Refrigerator Committee, 5 North Row, London W1, represents manufacturers of appliances and packaging and publishes free leaflets

FILMS
Freezeasy, a 20-minute, 16-mm film on packaging for the freezer, is loaned out free on receipt of £1·00 for postage and packing by Lakeland Plastics (see p. 90).

Courses

The Home Food Storage and Preservation section of the University of Bristol at Long Ashton Research Station holds two-day courses on freezing.

Many local education authorities hold further education courses on cooking for the freezer.

Glossary

Aluminium foil: a valuable packaging material for freezer storage. In sheet form, it can be moulded around food to exclude air. It is also available as rigid containers in assorted shapes for both cooking and freezer storage.

Ascorbic acid: also known as Vitamin C. This is the nutrient in fresh fruit and vegetables. The blanching of vegetables prevents it being destroyed. It is water soluble and easily oxidized. Obtainable from chemists, it can be added to the syrup when freezing some fruits, notably peaches, apples and plums, to prevent oxidation and subsequent browning.

Baking powder: a combination of chemicals, including cream of tartar and bicarbonate of soda, which is added to cakes to make them rise.

Battenberg: a two-coloured oblong sponge cake covered with almond paste.

Bay leaf: the aromatic leaf of the sweet bay tree. Used fresh or dried for flavouring.

Blanch: to scald vegetables in boiling water, thereby killing the enzymes that cause 'off' flavours; blanching also prevents the discolouration of fruits. All vegetables, and fruits that discolour, must be blanched before freezing.

Blast freezing: a method of freezing food commercially; food passing through a tunnel is subjected to very cold air which quick-freezes the food in minutes.

Bouquet garni: a bunch of herbs used in savoury dishes to give flavour. It consists of a sprig each of parsley and thyme and a bay leaf tied together in a piece of muslin. The bag is cooked with the food and removed before serving.

Charlotte: a pudding made with layers or a casing of cake or biscuits.

Citrus fruits: thick-skinned juicy fruits such as oranges, lemons, grapefruit, tangerines and satsumas.

Cling wrap: self-clinging plastic PVC film that moulds readily around objects and can create its own seal. The thinner type has a high oxygen permeability and needs over-wrapping for freezer use; the thicker 'freezer film' can be used on its own.

Cottage cheese: a soft cheese made from skimmed milk curds.

Cream cheese: cheese made from cream which has been allowed to sour then hung in muslin to drain.

Croûton: small cubes of bread that have been toasted or fried to use as a garnish for hot dishes or as an accompaniment for soup.

Curd cheese: similar to cottage cheese but usually smoother with medium-fat content.

Dehydration: also known as desiccation. The dry atmosphere of a freezer causes unwrapped food to dehydrate, or dry out, because the ice crystals that form as the food freezes evaporate, leaving the food dry and crumbly. Moisture-proof packaging is necessary to prevent dehydration, but if the packaging is pierced by some sharp object dehydration may occur in places. See *freezer burn*.

Dough: a thick mixture of uncooked flour and liquid, often combined with other ingredients.

Drip: the liquid that is released from frozen food as it thaws. A large quantity of drip denotes too slow a freezing process and too fast a thawing process, and the result will be dry food.

Enzyme: a protein that acts as a catalyst and is capable of speeding up chemical changes. Enzymes work more quickly in warm conditions and are destroyed by heat. Cold inhibits enzymic activity.

Flan: an open pastry case that can be filled with a sweet or savoury mixture and served either hot or cold.

Fast-freeze switch: also known as 'super-freeze' switch. The device on home freezers by which the thermostat may be isolated and continuous freezing power provided. It is unnecessary to operate the switch unless freezing over $\frac{1}{2}$kg (1 lb) of food at a time.

Freeze: to subject food to below-zero temperatures. On freezing, the moisture in the food forms ice crystals. If the freezing is slow, the crystals will be large and the food cells will be ruptured. Food is best quick-frozen.

Freezer burn: severe dehydration of the surface tissue

of frozen food. Correct packaging and sealing of food prevents freezer burn.

Game: wild animals or birds killed for food. Game is usually hung to tenderize the meat and develop the flavour; this must be done before freezing to have any effect.

Garlic: a plant of the onion family. The bulb is used for flavouring savoury dishes. The pungent flavour of garlic is spoiled by freezer storage, therefore it is best added to dishes after freezing.

Garnish: to add decorative touches to a savoury dish to improve its appearance; or, the decorative element itself. All garnishes should be edible and of a contrasting colour and texture to the dish. It is best to garnish dishes just before serving.

Gâteau: an elaborate cake, usually made from sponge or biscuit and cream or butter icing. Often served as a dessert.

Gelatine: a transparent, tasteless, water-soluble substance that sets jellies and thickens juices. See note on jelly on p. 35.

Glaze: any liquid used to give a glossy surface to sweet dishes, savouries and pastry.

Grade: to sort into even sizes.

Headspace: a space left at the top of containers of liquids for freezing, to allow for the expansion that occurs when liquids freeze and prevent the lid of the container being forced off. About 2 cm ($\frac{1}{2}$ in) headspace is adequate.

Hors d'oeuvres: light cold or hot snacks served at the beginning of a meal to stimulate the appetite.

Hull: to remove stalks and leaves from berry fruit.

Mature: to develop flavour, usually during storage.

Micro-organism: a minute form of life present in food. The three classes of micro-organism are moulds, yeasts and bacteria. Freezing greatly diminishes the activity of micro-organisms, which can spoil the flavour of stored food.

Oxidation: combination with oxygen, caused by enzymes. Browning of fruits is evidence of oxidation. The effect of oxidation can be minimized by covering the fruit with syrup and adding an anti-oxidant such as ascorbic acid (Vitamin C) or citric acid. When fats become oxidized they go rancid. This is why air (which contains oxygen) must be excluded from frozen food packages.

Pare: to shave off rind. Citrus fruits are often so treated because the pith immediately under the skin is bitter.

Pâté: a paste made from minced game, liver or fish, usually served as an hors d'oeuvres.

Pectin: the ingredient in fruits that maintains the fruit's structure. When pectin is boiled with the right proportion of acid and sugar it forms a gel which sets jams and jellies.

Poach: to cook food in a small quantity of water at a temperature just below boiling point. This gentle method of cooking prevents the food breaking up or toughening.

Pressure cooker: a large, heavy-duty, steamproof saucepan that provides a means of cooking food at a higher temperature than is possible by ordinary methods, and so greatly reduces the cooking time. Pressure cooking is particularly useful for foods that take a long time to cook.

Purée: a smooth pulp of vegetables, meat, fruit, etc. from which the fibrous elements have been removed by sieving.

Quiche: a savoury custard tart. The base of the filling is always an egg and cream or milk mixture, to which other ingredients may be added.

Ratatouille: a mixed vegetable stew that originated in Provence, France.

Sieve: to take out the fibrous part of food by pressing through a fine mesh.

Sift: to shake through a sieve, thus separating fine elements from coarse.

Simmer: to cook in a liquid from 85° to 91°C (185° to 195°F). Bubbles form slowly but collapse below the surface of the liquid.

Soft fruits: berries and currants; that is, those fruits with small pips and seeds, such as raspberries, strawberries, blackberries and black and red currants.

Sterilize: to kill the bacteria and enzymes that cause contamination. This is usually achieved by means of heat.

Sugar syrup: a liquid made by dissolving sugar in water, sometimes used for freezing fruit.

Terrine: an earthenware cooking dish used for cooking minced meats, in a form similar to pâté, which are served cold with toast; also, by extension, the meat itself.

Thaw: to return to an ambient temperature. Slow thawing of food—for example, in a refrigerator—enables the cells to re-absorb its moisture; thawed in this way, most foods will be moist and succulent (frozen vegetables, however, are best cooked from frozen).

Vacuum: a space entirely devoid of matter, in which bacteria and moulds that cause food spoilage cannot survive. Vacuum-packed foods are also protected from oxidation, so their storage life is increased.

Vitamin: a nutrient, present in many foodstuffs, which is essential to the healthy development of man and other animals. See also *ascorbic acid*.

Zest: the thin outer skin of citrus fruits.

Index

Credits

Artists
Ron Hayward Art Group
Oxford Illustrators
John Shackell

Photographs
Bryan Alexander, 5
Bird's Eye Foods, 8
Barry Bullough, 61, 73, 76, 81
Mary Evans Picture Library, 7
Food Freezer and Refrigerator Council, 9
Paul Kemp, 21, 44, 49, 57, 69
Octopus Books, 12

Cover
Photograph: Barry Bullough